THE NEW YORK PUBLIC LIBRARY AMAZING WORLD GEOGRAPHY

A Book of Answers for Kids

Andrea Sutcliffe

A Stonesong Press Book

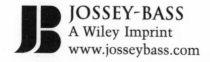

JOSSEY-BASS
A Wiley Imprint
www.josseybass.com

Published by Jossey-Bass
A Wiley Imprint
989 Market Street, San Francisco, CA 94103-1741   www.josseybass.com

All maps prepared by Netmaps, S.A.

Photo p. 66, Charles & Josette Lenars, CORBIS; p. 78, General Research Division, Humanities and Social Sciences Library, The New York Public Library, Astor, Lenox and Tilden Foundations; p. 92, Photography Collection, Humanities and Social Sciences Library, The New York Public Library, Astor, Lenox and Tilden Foundations; p. 102, Asian and Middle Eastern Division, Humanities and Social Sciences Library, The New York Public Library, Astor, Lenox and Tilden Foundations; p. 114, General Research Division, Humanities and Social Sciences Library, The New York Public Library, Astor, Lenox and Tilden Foundations

Readers should be aware that Internet Web sites offered as citations and/or sources for further information may have changed or disappeared between the time this was written and when it is read.

Jossey-Bass books and products are available through most bookstores. To contact Jossey-Bass directly call our Customer Care Department within the U.S. at 800-956-7739, outside the U.S. at 317-572-3986, or fax 317-572-4002.

Jossey-Bass also publishes its books in a variety of electronic formats. Some content that appears in print may not be available in electronic books.

ISBN 0-471-39296-0

Printed in the United States of America
FIRST EDITION
PB Printing   10 9 8 7 6 5 4 3 2

CONTENTS

INTRODUCTION

Why is geography important? For one thing, geography helps us to better understand the world we live in. It takes us out of our own neighborhoods and shows us where and how the world's other people live. Geography shows us the connections between people and places. Geography also describes how places on the earth change over time and how humans contribute to those changes. With this knowledge, geography lets us peer into the earth's future.

This book begins by giving you a geographic snapshot of the world as a whole, often using the United States as a point of comparison. It then takes you on a tour of the earth's seven continents and 191 countries. You'll learn about places and people, landscapes and languages. You'll learn about the largest and smallest, the highest and lowest, and the hottest and coldest. You'll learn which countries are growing, and which are shrinking, and why. You'll see how we depend on other parts of the world for so many of the products we use in our part of the world.

The questions here are just a start—the earth is way too big and interesting to be covered in one small book. We hope you'll soon be asking questions of your own. For answers, and to learn more about geography in general, we encourage you to visit the New York Public Library or your local library, and perhaps check out the geography resources listed at the back of this book.

Does the earth have six or seven continents? ◆ What is a
ectonic plate? ◆ Ha<del>ve the continents</del> always looked the
hey do today? ◆ Where is zero degrees latitude and zero
degrees longitude? ◆ W<del>hy do maps</del> always show the North
'ole at the top? ◆ How <del>old is the</del> earth? ◆ How far is it to
he center of the earth? ◆ Who owns the oceans? ◆ Which
s the largest oce<del>an in the world</del>? ◆ <del>What</del> is the world's
argest island? ◆ Is the pull of gravity the same all over the
earth? ◆ H<del>ow much of the earth is covered with</del> water? ◆
How muc<del>h of all the water on the earth is in the</del> oceans? ◆
Where is most of the earth's freshwater found? ◆ Where is
he world's wettest place? ◆ Where do most earthquakes

CHAPTER 1

THE WORLD AS A WHOLE

Does the earth have six or seven continents?

Traditionally, there are seven continents: North America, South America, Europe, Asia, Africa, Australia, and Antarctica. But there are just six distinct land masses because Europe and Asia lie on top of a single tectonic plate, called Eurasia.

The dividing line between the continents of Europe and Asia is usually the Ural Mountains in western Russia.

What is a tectonic plate?

The earth's crust is not one continuous shell, but instead is broken up into many pieces, which scientists call tectonic plates. No one is sure how many plates there are, but the number is probably between 20 and 40. The continents rest on top of these plates, and over millions of years the plates bearing the continents have been moving relative to one another.

When these plates bump into each other, earthquakes and volcanoes can occur and mountains may form. When the plates pull apart from each other, continents may break apart and oceans may form.

THE CONTINENTS

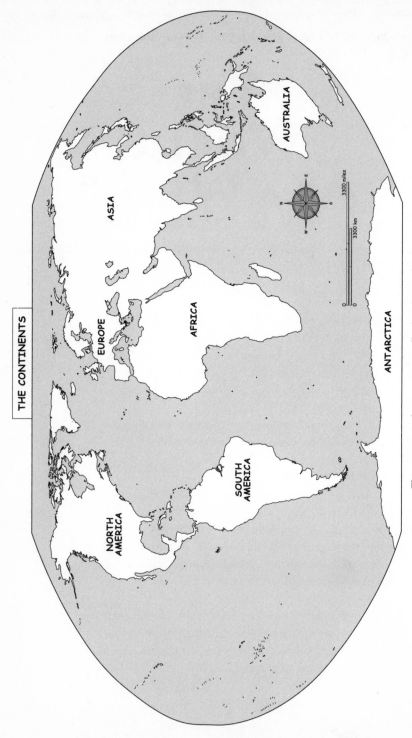

The seven continents are actually six separate land masses; Europe and Asia share the Eurasian tectonic plate.

Have the continents always looked the way they do today?

No, not according to the theory of continental drift. Scientists believe that early in the earth's history, there was just a single landmass, or continent, which they call Pangaea. About 200 million years ago, Pangaea broke up and the pieces began to drift.

Today's continent of Africa was at the center of Pangaea. South America broke off from southwestern Africa and drifted west, Antarctica broke away from Africa's southern tip and drifted south, and Australia broke off from Antarctica and headed east. North America split off from Africa's northwest coast and shifted west, and Eurasia broke off the top and moved north.

At one point, India split off from Africa's east coast and was an island for a long time, until it moved north into Asia, pushing against it so hard that the movement created the Himalayas. If you study the shapes of the continents on a map, you can see how their general outlines match up with one another.

The continents are still moving today.

The division of the supercontinent of Pangaea began roughly 200 to 225 million years ago. The continents as we know them today began forming then, and the tectonic plates that carry them continue to move.

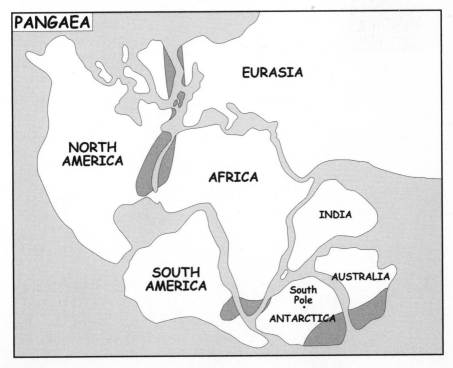

6   AMAZING WORLD GEOGRAPHY

Geographic Terms to Know

Northern Hemisphere: The half of the earth that lies north of the Equator, between 0° (the Equator) and 90° north latitude (the North Pole).

Southern Hemisphere: The half of the earth that lies south of the Equator, between 0° (the Equator) and 90° south latitude (the South Pole).

Equator: The imaginary line of 0° latitude that lies midway between the North and South poles.

Prime meridian: The imaginary line denoting 0° longitude that passes through the Royal Observatory in Greenwich, England.

Longitude: The distance east or west of the prime meridian, from 0° to 180° east or west. Lines of longitude run north–south.

Latitude: The distance north or south of the Equator, from 0° to 90° north or south. Lines of latitude run east–west and are parallel to each

other. Together, lines of latitude and longitude form a grid that lets us pinpoint exact locations on the earth's surface.

North Pole: The northern extremity of the earth's axis (the invisible line about which a body spins or rotates), and the northern point from which all meridians of longitude begin. The north polar region is made up of ice-covered ocean.

South Pole: The southern extremity of the earth's axis, and the southern center from which all meridians of longitude begin. The south polar region is made up of land.

Arctic Circle: The parallel of latitude that is about 66.5° north of the Equator that surrounds the north frigid zone.

Antarctic Circle: The parallel of latitude that is about 66.5° south of the Equator that surrounds the south frigid zone.

Where is zero degrees latitude and zero degrees longitude?

It's a point in the Atlantic Ocean, south of the African country of Ghana and west of another African country, Gabon. This is where the prime meridian and the Equator intersect.

Why do maps always show the North Pole at the top?

Not for any good reason. It's just been the way most map makers through time, most of whom have lived in the Northern Hemisphere, have shown the world on paper.

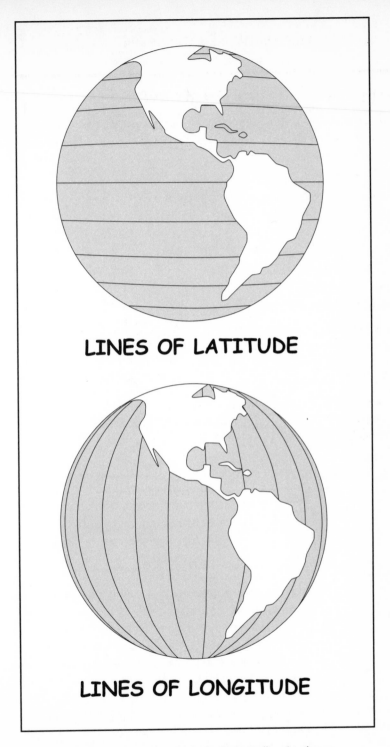

LINES OF LATITUDE

LINES OF LONGITUDE

Lines of latitude and longitude don't physically exist; they are concepts created by geographers and cartographers that make it easier for humans to describe locations on Earth.

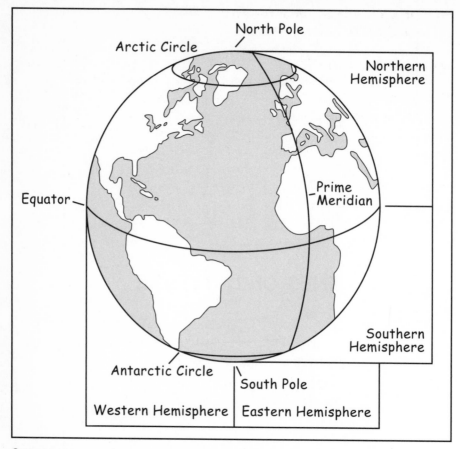

North Pole

Arctic Circle

Northern Hemisphere

Prime Meridian

Equator

Southern Hemisphere

Antarctic Circle

South Pole

Western Hemisphere | Eastern Hemisphere

Common geographic terms are illustrated above. Many are derived from ancient Greek words. For example, the word *hemisphere* means half a globe; thus the Northern Hemisphere refers to the northern half of the earth, the Southern Hemisphere means the southern half, and the Eastern and Western Hemispheres refer to the eastern and western halves of the globe.

How old is the earth?

Geologists estimate that the earth is about 4.6 billion years old. One way to tell the age of the earth is to figure out the age of the oldest rocks. In the very early days of our planet, molten rock, or magma, spread over the earth's surface and eventually cooled, forming the crust. Much of this rock has been buried or re-formed since that time, but some very old rocks can still be found.

The oldest known rocks are about 4 billion years old. These rocks, called tonalite gneiss, were found in 1999 north of Yellowknife in Canada's Northwest Territories. Other very old igneous rocks have been found in Greenland and Australia. Igneous rocks are those that formed from the hot molten material found deep below the earth's surface.

How far is it to the center of the earth?
It's about 3,700 miles (5,957 km).

Who owns the oceans?
Countries don't actually own the waters that surround them, but for centuries countries have claimed that certain distances off their shores belong to them. The usual distance was about 3 nautical miles. (A nautical mile is equivalent to about 1.15 land miles, or 1,852 meters.) The waters off a country's coastline are important not only because of fishing rights, but also because of the mineral and oil resources that may lie beneath the ocean floor.

In 1945, the United States began to claim its entire continental shelf—about 200 nautical miles off the Atlantic coast—as its territory. (A continental shelf is the underwater land that borders a continent.) Soon after, several South American countries claimed the same distances off their shores.

The United Nations has decided that all countries should have uniform limits on sea territories. No law has been passed yet, but most countries now agree on two limits: a 12-mile nautical sea zone, in which the country can enforce laws and exploit natural resources; and a 200-mile economic exploitation zone, in which the country can exploit, develop, manage, and conserve all the resources in the water, on the ocean floor, and in the subsoil. That covers everything from fish to oil and gas.

More than one-third of the world's people live within 60 miles of a coastline.

Which is the largest ocean in the world?
The Pacific Ocean is the largest by far. It's twice the size of the Atlantic Ocean, covering 64 million square miles (165.7 million sq km). It's also the deepest ocean. At the Mariana Trench, the deepest area of the Pacific, the seafloor is 36,198 feet (11,033 m)—almost 7 miles—below the surface.

The Pacific Ocean is so large that all the earth's continents could fit within its area with plenty of room left over. The Pacific Ocean holds almost half the world's water.

The Indian Ocean is almost as large as the Atlantic Ocean.

What is the world's largest island?
Greenland has 840,000 square miles (2,184,000 sq km), making it the largest island in the world. According

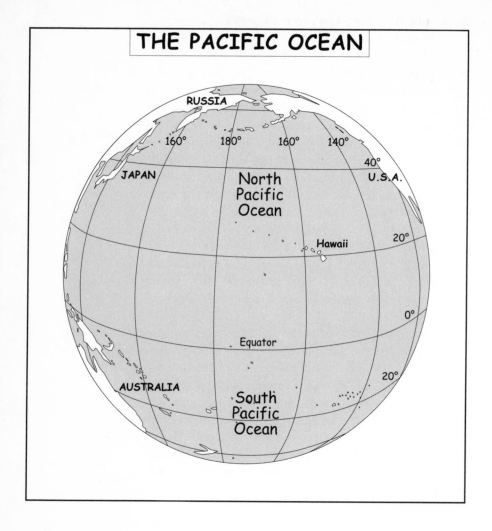

THE PACIFIC OCEAN

RUSSIA

160°   180°   160°   140°

40°

JAPAN   North   U.S.A.
               Pacific
               Ocean

                              Hawaii   20°

                                              0°

                    . Equator

                                              20°
AUSTRALIA

               ·South
               Pacific
               Ocean

A map of the earth showing the Pacific Ocean at its center reveals just how much of the earth's surface the Pacific covers.

to legend, it was named Greenland by its Norwegian discoverer, Erik the Red, in A.D. 985 because he wanted to encourage people to settle there. In truth, most of Greenland lies within the Arctic Circle and is partially green only for a short time in the summer.

Most of Greenland—nearly 85 percent—is covered with a huge ice sheet that averages about 5,000 feet (1,524 m) thick. From the island's northernmost point, the North Pole is only 500 miles (805 km) away.

Is the pull of gravity the same all over the earth?

Not quite. Although gravity is relatively the same everywhere, there are small variations. These are due to differences in density in the earth's mass. Scientists have recently discovered, with the help of two earth-orbiting satellites, that the pull of gravity is slightly less off the coast of India. They think this may be because of tectonic material left behind after the Indian subcontinent collided into the Eurasian tectonic plate millions of years ago. If you weigh 100 pounds in the United States, these scientists think you'd weigh about 1 percent, or about 1 pound, less in India.

How much of the earth is covered with water?

About 70 percent.

How much of all the water on the earth is in the oceans?

More than 97 percent of the earth's water is salty sea water. All of the earth's freshwater—water found in ice caps, lakes, rivers, and as groundwater (which is water found close to the surface, in wells and aquifers)—accounts for the remaining 3 percent.

Where is most of the earth's freshwater found?

Almost 70 percent of the all the freshwater in the world is frozen in Antarctica's and Greenland's ice caps. The other 30 percent is found in the atmosphere, streams, lakes, and groundwater.

The Great Lakes, in the United States and Canada, hold 6 quadrillion gallons of water and make up about one-fifth of the world's freshwater supply. Lake Baikal in Russia holds another one-fifth of the world's freshwater.

People in North America use eight times as much freshwater as people in Africa.

Where is the world's wettest place?

Lloro, Colombia, in South America receives the highest average annual precipitation in the world—an estimated 523.6 inches (1,330 cm) of rain a year, according to the U.S. National Oceanographic and Atmospheric Administration.

Where do most earthquakes happen?

Most earthquakes and volcanoes take place along plate boundaries—places where tectonic plates meet. One of the most active areas is around the Pacific Plate, known as the Ring of Fire.

Where did the most deadly earthquake in the world occur?

A terrible earthquake struck central China in 1557, killing about 830,000 people. Most died because they were living in caves made of soft rock, which collapsed during the quake. In more recent times, a 1976 earthquake in Tangshan, China, killed more than 250,000 people. It had a magnitude of 8.2.

What was the most powerful earthquake in the twentieth century?

A 1960 earthquake in southern Chile, along the coast of South America, had a magnitude of 9.5. The earthquake caused a tsunami, or huge wave, which destroyed several fishing villages on Chile's coastline and then raced across

The Ring of Fire

The Ring of Fire is home to more than half the world's 1,500 active volcanoes. Geologists use the term "active" to mean that a volcano may erupt again someday. Earthquakes are also common in the Ring of Fire.

Encircling most of the Pacific Ocean, the Ring of Fire extends from New Zealand in the South Pacific, north to Asia and Japan, across the northern Pacific to Alaska, and then south along the west coasts of North, Central, and South America.

Volcanoes are more likely to occur in these areas because the edges of the tectonic plates on which the Pacific Ocean sits are slowly pushing under other ocean plates or the plates of the surrounding continents. Geologists call this action subduction.

Subduction creates heat that melts materials inside the earth, creating magma. The magma weighs less than the rock that surrounds it, so eventually it rises and comes out of the earth in the form of lava—the hot molten rock that is spewed from volcanoes.

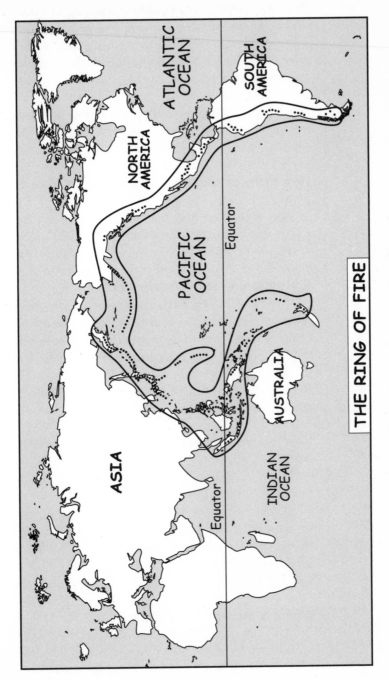

ASIA

NORTH
AMERICA

SOUTH
AMERICA

ATLANTIC
OCEAN

PACIFIC
OCEAN

INDIAN
OCEAN

AUSTRALIA

Equator

Equator

THE RING OF FIRE

The Ring of Fire surrounds the Pacific Ocean, and more than
half of the world's 1,500 active volcanoes are found there.

the Pacific Ocean. It struck Hilo, Hawaii, 14 hours later and continued on to the Philippines and Japan, causing more death and destruction. As many as 2,200 people may have died as a result of the earthquake and the tsunami. The earthquake also triggered the eruption of six volcanoes in Chile.

The next strongest earthquake of the twentieth century hit Alaska in 1964 with a magnitude of 9.2, killing 114 people.

How many earthquakes occur in the world each year?

Geologists estimate that about 500,000 earthquakes occur each year. Of these, about 100,000 are strong enough to be felt by people, and about 100 cause damage.

Can volcanoes form underwater?

Yes, and in fact most volcanoes are on the ocean floors, not on land. A chain of volcanoes below the sea circles the earth for more than 30,000 miles (48,300 km), standing, on average, about 18,000 feet (5,486 m) above the seafloor. This chain is called the Mid-Ocean Ridge. Here, tectonic plates are spreading apart and volcanoes are forming new crust.

How many volcanoes erupt each year all over the world?

About 60 volcanoes erupt somewhere on land every year. Many others erupt on the ocean floor.

About 50 volcanoes have been recorded as erupting in the United States (mainly in Oregon, Washington, Alaska, and Hawaii) since people started keeping track of such things. That makes the United States third in the world in volcanic activity, behind Indonesia and Japan.

Where is the world's largest volcano?

The largest volcano in the world is Mauna Loa in Hawaii. It rises about 56,000 feet (171 km) from its base, which is almost 5 miles (8 km) *below* the ocean floor, and covers almost half the island of Hawaii.

What was the deadliest volcano ever?

The Tambora volcano in Indonesia killed about 90,000 people in 1815. Most died of starvation and disease after the eruption. Crops and livestock were destroyed and the water became contaminated, leading to disease.

How many people have died from volcanoes during the past 500 years?

At least 300,000 people worldwide have died as result of volcanic activity since 1500, and many more lost their homes. Scientists estimate that volcanoes pose a risk to about 500 million people today.

Where is the largest mountain range in the world?

The world's greatest mountain range lies under the oceans. It's called the Mid-Ocean Ridge, and it runs for nearly 40,000 miles (64,374 km) from the Arctic to the Atlantic Oceans, around the continents of Africa, Asia, and Australia, then under the Pacific Ocean to the west coast of North America. Its tallest peak is 13,800 feet (4,200 m) above the ocean floor.

The largest mountain range on land is the Himalaya-Karakoram, which extends across India, Nepal, Sikkim, Bhutan, and Tibet in southern Asia. Of the world's highest 109 mountains, 96 are located there.

If measured from the seafloor, not from sea level, the tallest mountain in the world is Mauna Kea in Hawaii. It's 32,000 feet (9,754 m) high, measured from its base on the ocean floor to its peak.

What's the tallest mountain in the world?

Mount Everest, on the border of Nepal and Tibet in the Himalayan mountains, is tallest at 29,035 feet (8,850 m) above sea level. It was named for Sir George Everest, a British mountain climber. Its local name is Chomolungma, meaning "Goddess Mother of the World." The table on the right lists the five tallest mountains in the world.

Mountain peak	Range/ location	Height in feet (m)
Everest	Himalayas/ Nepal, Tibet	29,035 (8,850)
K2 (Godwin Austen)	Karakoram/ Pakistan, China	28,250 (8,611)
Kanchenjunga	Himalayas/ India, Nepal	28,169 (8,586)
Lhotse I	Himalayas/ Nepal, Tibet	27,940 (8,516)
Makalu	Himalayas/ Nepal, Tibet	27,766 (8,463)

What's the longest river in the world?

Africa's Nile River, which is 4,160 miles (6,693 km) long, is the longest. It flows through the countries of Uganda, Sudan, and Egypt.

The next longest is the Amazon River in South America, at 4,000 miles (6,436 km) long. It runs through the countries of Brazil, Peru, Colombia, Ecuador, Bolivia, and Venezuela. The Amazon carries more water than the Nile.

The third longest river is the Yangtze, or Chang, River in China, at 3,434 miles (5,525 km).

Where is the world's deepest lake?

The deepest lake in the world is Lake Baikal, in Russia's Siberia region. It is 5,369 feet (1,637 m) deep—more than 1 mile—and holds one-fifth of the world's freshwater. Scientists think that the lake is the oldest on the planet, at more than 25 million years old. It sits above a rift in the earth where three tectonic plates meet.

Lake Baikal is home to a large number of plants and animals, including 250 species of freshwater shrimp. One species of shrimp keeps the lake incredibly clear because it devours bacteria and algae. In recent years, the purity of the lake has been threatened by pollution from industrial plants on its shores.

Where is the world's largest lake?

The Caspian Sea, which is a saltwater lake that borders Russia, Kazakhstan, Turkmenistan, Azerbaijan, and Iran, covers 143,244 square miles (371,000 sq km). (See page 69 for more about the Caspian Sea.)

Where is the world's largest freshwater lake?

Lake Superior, one of the Great Lakes on the U.S.-Canadian border, covers 31,700 square miles (82,100 sq km).

Where is the world's highest waterfall?

Angel Falls in eastern Venezuela is the highest, with a drop of 3,212 feet (979 m) from Devil Mountain. That distance is more than twice the height of the Sears Tower in

Chicago, which is 1,450 feet (442 m) high. A U.S. pilot named Jimmy Angel discovered the falls by accident while searching for gold in 1935.

How much of the earth is covered by desert?

About one-third of all land surface is desert.

Where is the world's largest desert?

A desert is defined as a place that has little or no vegetation and receives less than 10 inches of precipitation a year. By that definition, the world's largest desert is most of Antarctica, about 5 million square miles (13 million sq km). Next is the Sahara Desert in northern Africa, which covers 3.5 million square miles (9 million sq km). The Sahara is 23 times larger than the Mojave Desert in California.

The highest temperature ever recorded on Earth was 136°F (58°C) at El Azizia, Libya, in Africa, in September 1922.

How many times does lightning strike around the world each day?

More than 86 million times a day, or about 100 lightning strikes every second.

Why are the seasons different in the Northern and Southern hemispheres?

Seasons differ because the earth is not upright on its axis in relation to the sun. Instead, it is tilted at about 23.5° from the vertical position relative to the sun. The earth revolves around the sun over the course of a year. When the earth's Southern Hemisphere is tilted toward the sun, the rays of the sun hit that part of the earth more

Disappearing Forests

More than half the forests that covered the earth 8,000 years ago are gone today. They've disappeared mostly because of human activities. For many hundreds of years, people have used wood for fuel and for building material.

Millions of trees were also cut down and cleared away to create farmland. Some scientists estimate that the planet is losing forests at the rate of 146 square miles (375 sq km) a day. That equals an area the size of Florida each year.

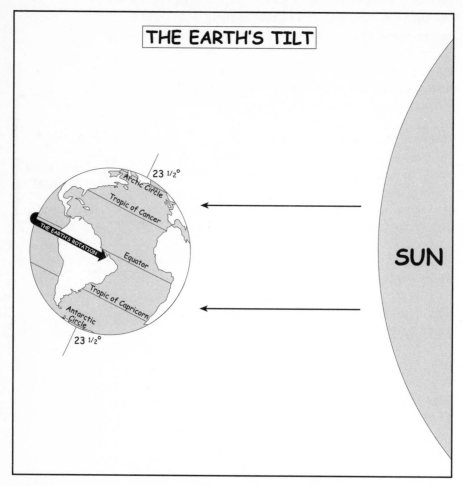

Because the earth tilts on its axis as it travels around the sun, only half the planet faces the sun directly at any one time. Thus, in July, when the Northern Hemisphere faces the sun, North America has summer weather, while South America is experiencing winter.

directly and cause warmer temperatures, resulting in summer weather. At the same time, the Northern Hemisphere is tilted away from the sun, so it receives fewer direct rays of the sun and experiences winter weather.

Why is it colder at the poles than at the equator?

As the earth orbits the sun, the sun's rays strike the areas near the Equator at a more direct angle—delivering more energy—than they do at the poles.

What's the world's largest country in land area?

Russia is the largest country, with 6.59 million square miles (17 million sq km). The next largest countries, in order, are Canada (3.83 million square miles), China (3.69

million square miles), the United States (3.68 million square miles), and Brazil (3.28 million square miles).

What's the world's smallest country in land area?

It's Vatican City, which is led by the Pope of the Roman Catholic Church. The country's official name is the Holy See of the Vatican City, and it is enclosed within Rome, Italy. About 1,000 people live there. The table on the right lists the world's five smallest countries.

1. Vatican City	0.2 square miles (0.4 sq km)
2. Monaco	0.6 square miles (1.9 sq km)
3. Nauru	8 square miles (21 sq km)
4. Tuvalu	10 square miles (26 sq km)
5. San Marino	24 square miles (61 sq km)

Which country has the longest coastline?

Canada's coastline is the world's longest, at 151,485 miles (243,792 km). That number includes the coastlines of the country's 52,455 islands.

How many countries are there in the world today?

The number depends on how "country" is defined. According to the U.S. State Department, there are 192 independent countries, if Taiwan is included. The problem is that China claims that Taiwan is a Chinese province, whereas Taiwan insists that it is an independent country. (See more about Taiwan on page 99.)

The United Nations has 190 members, but if you add the independent country that has chosen not to be a member—Vatican City—the total comes to 191. (The United Nations does not recognize Taiwan.)

The number of countries is constantly changing and has grown over the years. That's because so many national groups have broken away from their former countries and declared independence. In 1946, for example, there were just 74 countries.

How far do a country's boundaries extend?

A country's borders continue beneath the surface all the way to the earth's core. Above the ground, boundaries extend 100 miles (161 km) into the atmosphere. That

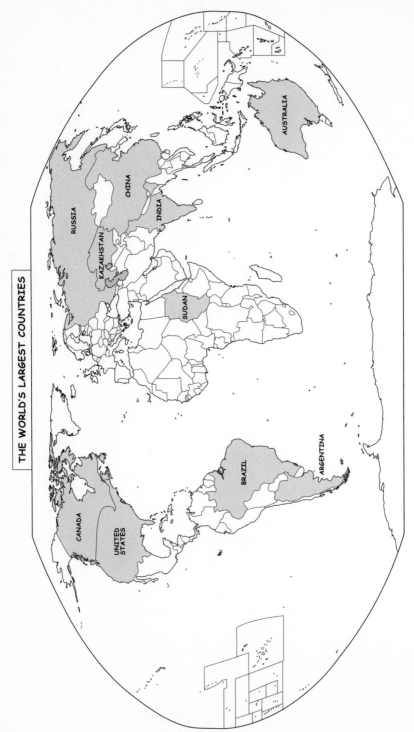

THE WORLD'S LARGEST COUNTRIES

The ten largest countries are shaded gray on this map.

RUSSIA

CHINA

INDIA

KAZAKHSTAN

AUSTRALIA

SUDAN

CANADA

UNITED STATES

BRAZIL

ARGENTINA

means that airlines must get permission to enter the air space of each country they fly over. (See the question about who owns the oceans on page 9 for more about country territories.)

Which countries are located on the Equator?

Starting in Africa and going east, they are Gabon, Republic of the Congo, Democratic Republic of the Congo, Uganda, Kenya, Somalia, Indonesia, Kiribati, Ecuador, Colombia, and Brazil.

Which countries are located at the prime meridian?

Going from north to south, they are the United Kingdom, France, Spain, Algeria, Mali, Burkina Faso, and Ghana.

Which countries have the most neighbors on their borders?

China and Russia border the most other countries, mainly because they both cover such large land areas. Each has 14 neighboring countries. Russia's borders touch Azerbaijan, Belarus, China, Estonia, Finland, Georgia, Kazakhstan, Latvia, Lithuania, Mongolia, North Korea, Norway, Poland, and Ukraine.

China is bordered by Afghanistan, Bhutan, India, Kazakhstan, Kyrgyzstan, Laos, Mongolia, Myanmar, Nepal, North Korea, Pakistan, Russia, Tajikistan, and Vietnam.

What does it mean when a country is landlocked?

A landlocked country is completely surrounded by land. That means it has no direct access to a sea or an ocean, an important advantage for trade. About one-fifth of the world's countries—42 to be exact—are landlocked. They must depend on their neighbors to give them access to the sea.

How many people live in the world today?

About 6.1 billion people lived on the planet in 2000. One out of every three people—more than 2 billion—live in just two countries: China and India.

1.	China	1.3 billion
2.	India	1 billion
3.	United States	281 million
4.	Indonesia	212 million
5.	Brazil	170 million
6.	Pakistan	150 million
7.	Russia	145 million
8.	Bangladesh	128 million
9.	Japan	126 million
10.	Nigeria	123 million

What is the world's largest country in population?

China had nearly 1.3 billion people in 2000. Nearly one out of every five people on Earth is Chinese. In 2000, the United States was the world's third largest country in population, but China still had more than four and a half times as many people. The table on the left lists the top 10.

What is meant by "the population explosion"?

In the twentieth century, the world's population grew at an amazing rate. In 1960, there were 3 billion people on Earth. Just 40 years later, the number of people more than doubled, to 6.1 billion.

In the 12 years between 1987 and 1999, the earth gained 1 billion people. Population experts predict that the population will grow by another 1 billion people—for a total of 7 billion—by around 2012. Then growth is expected to slow down a bit, as women in many countries start to have fewer children. By 2050, experts at the United Nations predict, there will be between 8 and 11 billion people on Earth. About that time, the population will begin to stabilize.

China and the United States cover about the same amount of land area.

Why will the world's population eventually stop growing?

The answer has to do with how many children are born each year. We know that children born today will have children in the future. So if fewer children are born today, fewer children will be born in the future.

In most countries of the world, women are having fewer children than their mothers did, and most population experts think this trend will continue. If, eventually, the average number of children born to each woman drops to 2.1—called the replacement level—the population will no longer grow. That's because those two children will exactly replace their mother and father.

Can you imagine 1 billion people? One way is to consider that 1 billion seconds equal 31.7 years.

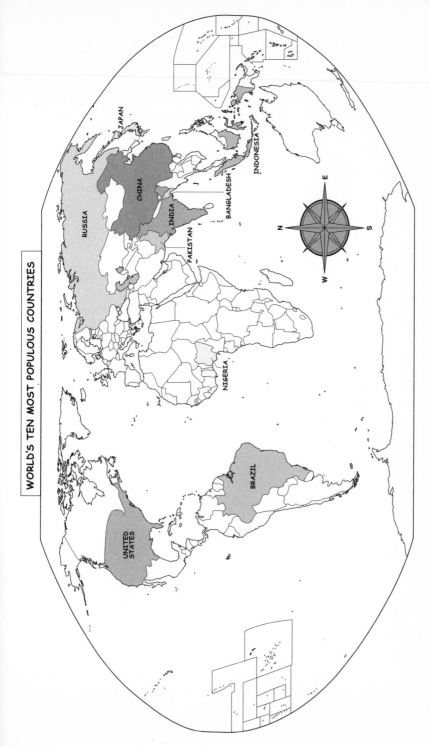

WORLD'S TEN MOST POPULOUS COUNTRIES

JAPAN
RUSSIA
CHINA
INDIA
PAKISTAN
BANGLADESH
INDONESIA
NIGERIA
BRAZIL
UNITED STATES

N
E
W
S

Seven of the world's most populous countries are in Asia, and many of them are growing rapidly.

When did the world population first reach 1 billion people?

The world population reached 1 billion for the first time in 1804. It then took 123 years for the number of people to *double,* to 2 billion, in 1927. It took just 72 years for that number to *triple,* to 6 billion people, in 1999.

In 2000, one out of every three people in the world was under the age of 15— that's about 1.8 billion kids.

How many people have ever lived on Earth?

Demographers—people who study population—have estimated that since 50,000 B.C., a total of 105 billion people have lived on Earth. That means about 5.5 percent of everyone who has ever lived is alive today.

What's the most crowded country in the world?

The most densely populated country in the world is Monaco, with more than 55,000 people per square mile.

Singapore, a city-state where 4 million people live on an island of 239 square miles (621 sq km), has a population density of 16,736 people per square mile. Malta has 3,076 people per square mile. Other crowded countries are Bahrain, Maldives, and Bangladesh.

Of the world's more than 6 billion people, nearly 1 billion cannot read or sign their names.

Which parts of the world are growing the fastest?

Almost all of the world's rapid population growth—about 99 percent—is happening in poor, less developed countries in Africa, Asia, and Latin America. About 4.9 billion of the world's 6.1 billion people—or about five of every six people on the planet—live in those areas.

India will probably have more people than China by 2050 because women in India are having more children than women in China.

Which countries are growing the fastest?

Just six countries account for *half* the world's annual growth of 77 million people each year: India, China, Pakistan, Nigeria, Bangladesh, and Indonesia, in that order.

Which parts of the world are growing more slowly?

Many countries in Europe—including Italy, Germany, and Russia—are actually losing population because women there are having fewer children than ever before. Japan is also shrinking in population.

The United States would be growing more slowly if it weren't for immigration—people moving there from other countries. This is also true for Australia, New Zealand, and Canada.

Only 1.1 billion of the world's 6.1 billion people live in Europe, Canada, the United States, Australia, and New Zealand.

What are the largest cities in the world in population?

The list below gives the populations of the largest metropolitan areas (including the central city and its surrounding areas) in 2000.

In 2000, half the people in the world lived in urban areas. The percentage of city dwellers is growing every year.

1.	Tokyo, Japan	33.1 million
2.	New York City, United States	21.1 million
3.	Seoul-Inchon, South Korea	19.9 million
4.	Mexico City, Mexico	18.1 million
5.	São Paulo, Brazil	17.7 million
6.	Mumbai (Bombay), India	17.5 million
7.	Osaka-Kōbe-Kyoto, Japan	16.9 million
8.	Los Angeles, United States	16.0 million
9.	Manila, Philippines	14.1 million
10.	Cairo, Egypt	14.0 million

What cities will be the world's largest in population in 2015?

In this order, the largest cities in population will be Tokyo, Japan; Mumbai (Bombay), India; and Lagos, Nigeria.

In 1960, New York City was the largest city in the world.

WORLD'S TEN LARGEST CITIES IN POPULATION

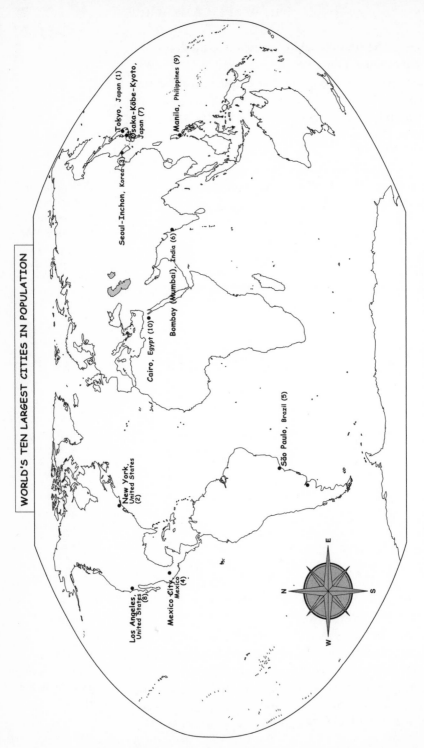

The world's most populous cities are fairly evenly distributed around the world, with four in North and South America, one in Africa, and five in Asia.

Tokyo, Japan (1)
Osaka–Kōbe–Kyoto, Japan (7)
Manila, Philippines (9)
Seoul–Inchon, Korea (3)
Bombay (Mumbai), India (6)
Cairo, Egypt (10)
São Paulo, Brazil (5)
New York, United States (2)
Los Angeles, United States (8)
Mexico City, Mexico (4)

What were the world's largest cities in population 1,000 years ago?

The world in the year 1000 was much smaller and quite different from the world today. The list below shows the world's biggest cities (and their estimated populations) at that time:

1.	Cordova, Spain	450,000
2.	Kaifeng, China	400,000
3.	Constantinople (Istanbul), Turkey	300,000
4.	Angkor, Cambodia	200,000
5.	Kyoto, Japan	175,000
6.	Cairo, Egypt	135,000
7.	Baghdad, Iraq	125,000
8.	Nishapur (Neyshabur) Iran	125,000
9.	Al-Hasa, Saudi Arabia	100,000
10.	Patan (Anhilwara), India	100,000

What is the difference between a nation and a state?

First, there are two kinds of "states." One is a division of a country, as in the 50 states of the United States. The other kind of state is any country. By definition, a country must occupy a space with internationally recognized boundaries, and it must be a self-governing political entity, among other things.

A nation, however, is slightly different. It is defined as a tightly knit group of people who share a common language, institutions, religion, and historical experience. Most countries are nation-states, including the United States, Germany, and France, for example. Canada, though, is one state with two nations—the British and the French cultures.

A nation can exist without having a state or a country. One example is the Palestinians. Palestine is not an independent country, although the Palestinian people would like to have their own state.

Another example is the Basque nation in southwestern Europe. For longer than anyone knows, the Basque people have lived in the western foothills of the Pyrenees mountains, the border area of France and Spain. Today, most of the more than 2 million Basques live in Spain. For years, many Basques have wanted to form their own country, separate from Spain and France.

The Basque language, called Euskera, is one of the most mysterious and oldest on earth—it is not related to any other known language. Genetic studies of the Basque people have shown that they are not related to any other European peoples.

Where in the world do people live the longest?

Today, girls born in Japan can expect to live to be 84, the longest life expectancy in the world. Girls born in Switzerland are next; they can expect to live to age 83. Girls born today in Australia, Iceland, Sweden, and France have a life expectancy of 82 years. Girls born today in the United States can expect to live to age 80.

Boys born in Japan, Sweden, Iceland, and Switzerland today can expect to live to age 77, the longest life expectancy for males in the world. Boys born today in the United States can expect to live to age 74.

Humans depend on just 20 plant species for more than 80 percent of their food. And half the daily calories consumed worldwide come from just three grains: wheat, rice, and corn.

How many of the world's people go hungry every day?

About 840 million, or one of every 14 people on the earth, don't have enough to eat, according to the United Nations. Most live in developing countries in Africa and in the Asia-Pacific region. India alone has about 202 million people who do not get enough food. Poverty is the main reason people go hungry.

How many languages are spoken in the world today?

No one knows for sure, but the number is probably between 6,000 and 7,000 languages, plus many more

Focus on World Poverty

- Every day, 34,000 children under age five die from hunger or related causes. That means one child dies every 2.5 seconds, every day.

- About one out of every four people on Earth live in poorly built homes with poor sanitation and an irregular supply of electricity—if they have electricity at all. Another 100 million people—one out of 60—have no housing at all.

- One out of every three people lacks access to safe water and sanitation systems.

dialects (a regional version of a language with different pronunciations, accents, and words). Most of these languages have relatively few speakers.

Every year, languages are dying out as technology and industry move into parts of the world that were once isolated. Some experts predict that a hundred years from now, as many as 90 percent of the languages spoken today will be close to extinction or already extinct. Most of these lost languages will be in Africa and Indonesia.

What are the most widely spoken languages in the world?

Mandarin Chinese tops the list, with about 885 million people who speak it as a first language. Here's a list of the top 10 languages and the countries or regions in which each is a leading language:

On average, one world language begins to die out every 10 days because children are no longer speaking or learning it.

1. Mandarin Chinese: China, Taiwan, Singapore
2. Spanish: Spain, parts of North, Central, and South America
3. English: Great Britain, the United States, Canada, Australia, New Zealand, numerous former British colonies in Asia and Africa
4. Bengali: Bangladesh, eastern India
5. Hindi: India
6. Portuguese: Portugal, Brazil
7. Russian: Russia, several former Soviet republics

8. Japanese: Japan

9. German: Germany, Austria, Switzerland, Luxembourg

10. Wu Chinese: China

What is Esperanto?

Esperanto is a made-up, or artificial, language devised by a Polish doctor named Ludovic L. Zamenhof about 100 years ago to serve as a common language between people who speak different native languages. Its words are based on common words in European languages, and it is fairly easy to learn because its grammar rules are simple and its words are spelled the way they are pronounced. No one knows for sure how many people use Esperanto—estimates range from 100,000 to 2 million people. Most live in central and eastern Europe and in eastern Asia.

Which are the world's most widely practiced religions?

The top three world religions are Christianity, Islam, and Buddhism. Together, about half the world's people follow the beliefs and teachings of these religions. Islam is the fastest growing of the three.

Christianity has the most followers, nearly 2 billion, and they live mainly in North America, South America, and Europe. About half of all Christians are Roman Catholic.

Almost a billion Muslims, or people who practice Islam, live mainly in Indonesia, Bangladesh, India, Pakistan, Saudi Arabia, Iran, Iraq, several other Middle Eastern countries, and northern Africa.

Most Buddhists live in China, Korea, Japan, and other Asian countries.

Where do most of the world's Jewish people live?

The United States is home to the largest concentration of Jewish people in the world, with about 5.8 million. Next is Israel, with 4.6 million, followed by Russia, France, Ukraine, Canada, and Great Britain.

About as many people speak Korean as a first language as speak French—between 70 and 75 million. Spanish and English also have nearly the same number of primary speakers—at 332 million for Spanish and 322 million for English.

Judaism, Christianity, and Islam all began in the Middle East, and they share many of the same beliefs and prophets.

The massive movement of Jews all over the world since the end of World War II is called the Jewish diaspora. Many Jews left Europe to seek a better life in other parts of the world. For example, almost 1.5 million Jews left Russia for other countries between 1948 and 1996.

Which is the richest country in the world?

The United States is the world's richest country, followed by Japan. Economists measure a country's wealth by looking at the total value of the goods and services it produces each year. They call this the GNP, which stands for gross national product. In 2000, the United States had the world's highest GNP by far—nearly $9 trillion. Japan was second, with $4 trillion, followed by Germany, France, the United Kingdom, and Italy.

Another way to measure wealth is to divide a country's GNP by the number of people who live in that country. This is called the GNP per capita. Using this measure, the world's richest country is Luxembourg, not the United States. The next richest countries in GNP per capita are Switzerland, Norway, Denmark, Japan, and Singapore. The United States ranks seventh.

Of the world's 6 billion people, 1.2 billion live on the equivalent of a dollar a day or less.

Which country consumes the most electricity in the world?

The United States tops the list—it generates and consumes about one-fourth of all the electricity worldwide. China is second, consuming about one-tenth of the world's electricity, followed by Russia, Japan, Germany, India, and Canada, in that order.

The average person in the United States uses 23 times as much fossil fuel energy as the average person in India.

Which country is the world's worst air polluter?

The United States is the world's leading air polluter, responsible for one-fourth of all carbon dioxide emissions. Carbon dioxide emissions result from burning fossil fuels, such as gasoline, oil, natural gas, and coal. China is the world's second worst air polluter, accounting for 12 percent of carbon dioxide emissions, followed by Russia, Japan, Indonesia, and India.

Most of these emissions result from industrial activity. However, automobile emissions send large amounts of

In the United States, there are 750 motor vehicles for every 1,000 people. In China, there are eight vehicles for every 1,000 people.

The warmest 10 years of the twentieth century all happened between 1985 and 2000.

The Middle East has 10 times more oil reserves than North America. The numbers, in billions of barrels, are 684 for the Middle East and 64 for North America.

Added together, the Middle East countries and the countries of the former Soviet Union hold more than 70 percent of the world's reserves of natural gas. Only 7 percent of the world's reserves of natural gas are in North America.

carbon dioxide into the atmosphere, and the United States has more cars than any other country in the world.

As China, Russia, and other industrialized countries continue to expand their economies, their percentage of carbon emissions will increase. Many experts say that carbon emissions are causing the average temperatures on Earth to rise, a phenomenon known as global warming.

Why is global warming considered to be a bad thing?

One of the biggest concerns about global warming is that higher temperatures could affect food production in many parts of the world. Many crops need certain temperature ranges to grow properly. Food shortages and famine could result. Also, if warmer temperatures cause polar ice to melt, sea levels could rise and lead to flooding in coastal areas.

How much oil is left in the world?

Humans have already used up about one-third of the world's known oil reserves, and scientists predict that there is only enough oil to sustain current levels of production for perhaps another hundred years.

Oil is distributed unevenly over the earth. Almost 80 percent is in the Eastern Hemisphere, and most of that is in the Middle East. Only about 17 percent of known oil reserves are in North America, Western Europe, and Central and South America.

How much gold has been mined so far in the world?

More than 193,000 metric tons. If you could take all of this gold and shape it into a solid cube, each side of the cube would be 72 feet (22 m) high. South Africa, the United States, and Australia lead the world in gold production.

How much silver has been mined so far in the world?

Much more silver than gold has been mined—more than 1,740,000 metric tons. It would form a cube 180 feet

(55 m) high on each side. Most of the world's silver comes from Mexico and Peru.

How many people in the world use the Internet?

One estimate is that 600 million people were using the Internet by 2002. In 2001, there were more than 500 million users worldwide. The United States leads in total number, with about 4 of every 10 people using the Internet. But as a percentage of the total population, more people in Canada, Sweden, and Finland log on to the Net than in the United States.

How many computers are in use in the world today?

Almost 600 million computers were working in the world in 2000. The country with the most computers is the United States, with more than 164 million, followed by Japan, Germany, the United Kingdom, France, Italy, Canada, China, Australia, and South Korea, in that order.

Where are the world's tallest buildings?

In 2000, the tallest buildings in the world were the Petronas Twin Towers in Kuala Lumpur, Malaysia. The towers are each 88 stories and 1,483 feet (452 m) tall.

But at least two other buildings are under construction that will be taller. The World Financial Center in Shanghai, China, will have 94 stories and rise to 1,509 feet (460 m). The 1,884-foot (574 m) Kowloon Mass Transit Railway Tower is being built in Hong Kong.

Where is the world's longest suspension bridge?

In Japan—the Akashi Kaikyo Bridge connecting the city of Kōbe with Awaji Island over the Akashi Strait opened in 1998 and is 2.43 miles (3.9 km) long. The main span is 1.24 miles (2 km) long. All four of Japan's main islands are now connected by bridges.

Because the bridge is near the epicenter of the earthquake that hit Kōbe in 1995, its designers made sure that its foundations were deep enough to withstand earthquakes up to a magnitude of 8.5 on the Richter scale.

The previous record holder was the Humber Estuary Bridge in Humberside, Great Britain, which has a 4,625-foot (1,410-m) main span.

Where is the world's longest subway system?

The London Underground—nicknamed the Tube—is the world's longest subway system. It has 244 miles (391 km) of track.

Where is the world's longest railroad tunnel?

Japan's Seikan Tunnel is 33 miles (53 km) long and connects the main Japanese island of Honshū with the northern island of Hokkaidō. The tunnel extends for 14.5 miles (23 km) under water.

Where is the world's busiest seaport?

Rotterdam, Netherlands, is the world's busiest port city. It handles more than 325 million tons (296 metric tons) of cargo annually. The world's second busiest seaport is the Port of South Louisiana in New Orleans, followed by the ports of Singapore, Kōbe (Japan), and Shanghai (China).

Where is the world's busiest airport?

O'Hare International Airport in Chicago, Illinois, is the world's busiest passenger airport. It beat out the previous world's busiest airport, Hartsfield International Airport in Atlanta, Georgia, in 2001. O'Hare had 911,861 takeoffs and landings in 2001.

The busiest cargo airport in the world is in Memphis, Tennessee, which happens to be the hub for Federal Express.

CHAPTER 2

NORTH AND CENTRAL AMERICA

Where did the first people in North America come from?

Scientists believe that many, if not all, of the first people in North America came from Asia. About 12,500 years ago, they left what is now Siberia and walked over the Bering Land Bridge (now covered by water and called the Bering Strait) to Alaska.

The descendants of these first people may have eventually spread out into all parts of North and Central America, possibly reaching South America.

But some scientists are beginning to think that the Bering Land Bridge was not the only route to the Americas. Remarkably, some people may have arrived by boat thousands of years before others walked across to Alaska. They probably came at different times and from across both the Pacific and Atlantic Oceans to both North and South America.

Is Greenland part of North America?

Yes, geographically. But politically Greenland is a self-governing province that belongs to Denmark, a European nation. Greenland is the largest island in the world. Its official name is Kalaallit Nunaat in the Greenlandic language. Most of its 57,000 citizens are of Inuit and Danish ancestry.

One of every eight people in the world lives in North America.

North America is the only continent that experiences all of the earth's climate groups: tropical, mild, continental, dry, high elevation, and polar.

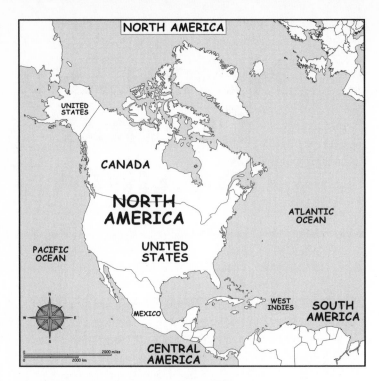

The continent of North America technically includes Central America and the islands of the West Indies.

Is Greenland close to Canada?

Yes, at its closest point Greenland is only 10 miles (16 km) from Canada. Most of Greenland lies north of the Arctic Circle. At its northernmost point, Greenland is only 440 miles (708 km) from the North Pole.

Does it get warm in Greenland in the summer?

The warmest place in Greenland is along the southwestern coast, location of the capital city, Godthab. In July, high temperatures average about 50°F (10°C).

Why isn't Greenland considered a continent, like Australia?

Geographers have decided that Greenland is too small to be called a continent. Australia is three and a half times larger.

Where was the world's tallest iceberg spotted?

The world's tallest iceberg was measured off the coast of Greenland in 1958: it was 550 feet (168 m) high. That's about the same height as the Washington Monument in Washington, D.C. About one-fifth to one-eighth of a typical iceberg protrudes above the surface of the water.

Who were the ancestors of most people living in North America today?

Most people in Canada, the United States, Mexico, and Central America are descended from Europeans. Spain had colonies in Mexico, Cuba, and Central America, so most of the people there can claim Spanish ancestors.

The United States was colonized by Great Britain, but in the 1800s and 1900s, people from many countries in Europe, Asia, and Central America immigrated to the United States as well. Today, only about one out of every three U.S. citizens is of British descent.

Canada was colonized by both Great Britain and France, but it has received immigrants from many other European and Asian countries during the past century. Today, about one-fourth of all Canadians have British ancestors, and one-fourth are of French descent.

When did the first Europeans settle in North America?

Archaeologists believe that the 1,000-year-old Viking settlement at L'Anse aux Meadows, Newfoundland—a province of Canada—is the oldest in North America. Led by Leif Eriksson, the Vikings who settled there called it Vinland.

What are the names of Canada's 10 provinces?

Going from west to east, they are British Columbia, Alberta, Saskatchewan, Manitoba, Ontario, Quebec, Newfoundland, New Brunswick, Prince Edward Island, and Nova Scotia. Canada also has three territories: Yukon Territory, Northwest Territories, and Nunavut. The provinces span six time zones.

Where is Nunavut?

Nunavut can't be found on older maps because it is a new Canadian territory. It was carved out of the eastern part of the Northwest Territories on April 1, 1999, and it is

Canada holds 9 percent of the world's freshwater supply, but it is home to only 1 percent of the world's population. Lakes and wetlands cover about 20 percent of Canada.

Canada occupies 50 percent of North America and nearly 7 percent of the earth's surface.

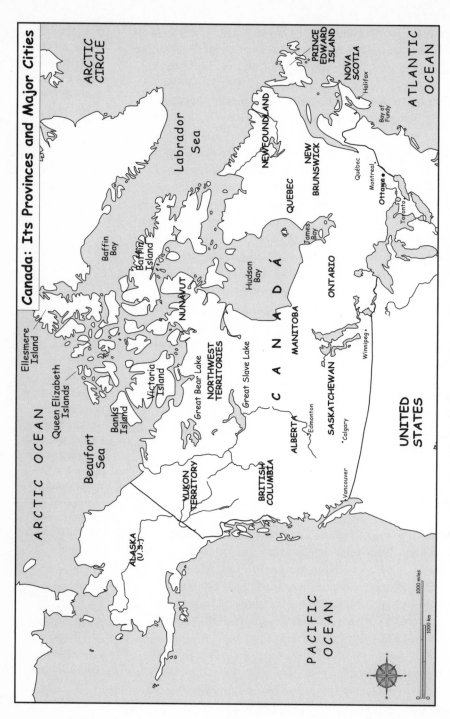

Canada: Its Provinces and Major Cities

This map shows Canada's 10 provinces and three territories, including its newest territory, Nunavut, separated from the Northwest Territories in 1999.

ARCTIC CIRCLE

ARCTIC OCEAN

Ellesmere Island

Queen Elizabeth Islands

Banks Island

Victoria Island

Baffin Bay

Baffin Island

Labrador Sea

NUNAVUT

NEWFOUNDLAND

PRINCE EDWARD ISLAND

NOVA SCOTIA

Halifax

ATLANTIC OCEAN

Bay of Fundy

Beaufort Sea

Great Bear Lake

NORTHWEST TERRITORIES

Great Slave Lake

Hudson Bay

James Bay

QUEBEC

NEW BRUNSWICK

Québec

Montreal

Ottawa

Toronto

YUKON TERRITORY

ALASKA (U.S.)

BRITISH COLUMBIA

ALBERTA

Edmonton

Calgary

SASKATCHEWAN

MANITOBA

Winnipeg

ONTARIO

C A N A D A

Vancouver

UNITED STATES

PACIFIC OCEAN

1000 miles

1000 km

38

the first self-governing Native American territory in North America. Nunavut is an Inuit word meaning "Our Land."

Nunavut occupies one-fifth of Canada's total land area but it has only about 22,000 people. Most of its residents are Inuits, who used to be called Eskimos. Its capital is Iqaluit, which lies three degrees south of the Arctic Circle.

What are the largest Canadian cities in population?

Toronto is the largest, with about 2.39 million people living in its metropolitan area. The next largest cities are Montréal, Vancouver, Ottawa-Hull, Edmonton, Calgary, and Winnipeg, in that order.

Is most of Canada covered with snow in the winter?

Yes. Except for coastal areas of British Columbia in the western part of the country, most of Canada has continuous snow cover in the winter, and average temperatures stay below freezing. But Canada—because it is so large—has many different climate types.

The climate on the Pacific Coast is similar to that of Great Britain: wet with moderate temperatures both winter and summer. In the north, winters are long and cold and summers are short and cool. The south-central plains area, as well as Ontario and Quebec, have a climate similar to the midwestern United States—cold winters and hot, humid summers.

Are all of the Great Lakes in Canada?

No, Lake Michigan lies completely within the United States. The United States and Canada each have boundaries on the other four Great Lakes: Superior, Huron, Erie, and Ontario.

Do Canadians celebrate Thanksgiving Day?

Yes, but their Thanksgiving is on the second Monday in October, not the fourth Thursday in November, as in the United States, because harvest time comes earlier in Canada. Canadians do enjoy turkey, mashed potatoes, and pumpkin pie on Thanksgiving, but they don't associate their holiday with pilgrims and the landing of the *Mayflower*. Instead, they refer back to the landing of

The north magnetic pole—the point toward which a compass needle points—is located in Nunavut's Elizabeth Islands, at about 77° north latitude, 102° west longitude.

One of the tallest free-standing structures in the world is the CN Tower in Toronto, at 1,815 feet (553 m).

Eight of Canada's 20 largest cities are located along the shores of the Great Lakes.

The province of Ontario is the only province to touch all four of the Great Lakes that border Canada.

Martin Frobisher from England at what is now Newfoundland in 1578, 43 years before the pilgrims landed in Massachusetts.

Is English Canada's official language?

It is one of them. Canada has two official languages: English and French. About 17 million of Canada's 28.5 million people claim English as their first language. Nearly 7 million speak French, most of whom live in the province of Quebec. Canada is home to 5 million immigrants as well, and many of them primarily speak their native languages—the most common are Chinese, Italian, and German. Very few Canadians speak Native American or Inuit languages because those groups make up less than 3 percent of the population.

Most of Canada is so cold and barren that three-quarters of its people live within 100 miles of the U.S. border. About 89 percent of Canada has never been permanently settled.

Does Canada belong to the United Kingdom?

No, Canada has been an independent country since 1931. But it is still a member of the British Commonwealth—also called the Commonwealth of Nations—which is made up of the United Kingdom and several countries that used to be part of the British Empire. Membership is voluntary, and its members share trade, investment, and social interests. Commonwealth nations are self-governing and acknowledge the British king or queen as a symbolic leader only.

Does Canada have a president and a congress like the United States?

No, the Canadians are led by a prime minister, who is the leader of the political party that wins the most seats in its parliament. The parliament of Canada consists of the Senate and the House of Commons. The 104 senators are appointed by the 10 provincial governments, and they may serve until they are 75 years old. The 301 members of the House of Commons are elected by the people and serve up to 5 years.

Is "Canada" an Indian name?

Yes, it probably comes from the Iroquois word *kanata,* meaning "villages" or "settlement."

What is the longest river in Canada?

The Mackenzie River, in the Northwest Territories, is 2,635 miles (4,241 km) long—almost 300 miles longer than the Mississippi River in the United States. It is named for the explorer Alexander Mackenzie, who was the first person to cross Canada and reach the Pacific in 1793.

Three of the world's 10 largest islands are in Canada: Baffin Island, Ellesmere Island, and Victoria Island.

Which river is sometimes called the Mother of Canada?

The St. Lawrence River, because this 800-mile-long (1,300 km) river was so important to explorers, fur traders, and settlers in the early years of Canada's history. Today, the St. Lawrence River, which forms part of the St. Lawrence Seaway, is still important to Canada and the United States because it is a direct route for freighters between the Great Lakes and the Atlantic Ocean. The St. Lawrence Seaway consists of some 9,500 miles of navigable waterways in the Great Lakes–St. Lawrence system.

What is Canada's highest mountain?

Mount Logan, in the southwestern Yukon Territory near Alaska, is 19,525 feet (5,951 m) above sea level.

What are Canada's most important agricultural products?

Canadian farmers produce wheat, barley, corn, flaxseed, and canola, as well as beef cattle, hogs, poultry, and dairy products. Most of the country's farms and ranches are located in the prairie provinces of Saskatchewan, Alberta, and Manitoba.

The fishing industry is important to communities throughout the Atlantic provinces of Newfoundland, New Brunswick, Prince Edward Island, and Nova Scotia and in the Pacific province of British Columbia.

Canada exports more forestry products than all its farm and fishery products combined. It leads the world in pulp and paper exports, and it sends much of its lumber to the United States. Forests cover almost half of Canada.

Where is the world's longest highway?

The longest national highway in the world is the Trans-Canada Highway. It connects Victoria, British

Columbia, on the west coast with St. John's, Newfoundland, on Canada's east coast, a distance of about 5,000 miles (8,000 km). It was built in just 15 years, from 1950 to 1965.

Is it true that the world's largest shopping mall is in Canada?

Yes. West Edmonton Mall in Edmonton, Alberta, has more than 800 stores, 100 restaurants, six amusement attractions, and a 335-room hotel. The next biggest shopping mall in North America is the Mall of America, in Bloomington, Minnesota.

How many U.S. states lie on the 5,527-mile (8,895-km) border with Canada?

Twelve states border Canada: Alaska, Washington, Idaho, Montana, North Dakota, Minnesota, Wisconsin, Michigan, New York, Vermont, New Hampshire, and Maine. It is the longest undefended border in the world.

Is Niagara Falls in the United States or Canada?

Both. The Niagara River forms part of the U.S.–Canada border. There are two falls on the Niagara River—the American Falls in New York State and the Horseshoe Falls in Canada. All but about 6 percent of the water flows over Horseshoe Falls, which is 158 feet (48 m) high. The highest waterfall in Canada is Della Falls in British Columbia, at 1,443 feet (440 m).

In 2000, the United States was the world's third largest country, with more than 281 million people. China (1.3 billion people) and India (1 billion people) are much larger. In land area the United States is the fourth largest country, after Russia, Canada, and China.

What is the distance between the United States and Russia at the closest point?

It's 51 miles (82 km) between Cape Dezhnyov, Russia, and Cape Prince of Wales, Alaska—the narrowest part of the Bering Strait. The Bering Strait connects the Bering Sea—which is part of the Pacific Ocean—with the Arctic Ocean, and it separates Asia and North America.

How long did it take to build the Alaska Highway?

It took engineers less than a year to build this 1,397-mile (2,248-km) road from Dawson Creek, British

Columbia, in Canada, to Delta Junction, Alaska (near Fairbanks) during 1942 and 1943. They were in a hurry because a route was needed during World War II to transport military supplies to U.S. bases in Alaska. A few sections of the highway are still gravel-surfaced today.

What is the highest mountain in the United States?

Mount McKinley in Alaska (also called Denali, its Native American name) is the highest, at 20,320 feet (6,194 m); it's also the highest mountain in North America. The next 16 highest peaks in the United States are also in Alaska. Ranked at number 18 is Mount Whitney in California, at 14,494 feet (4,418 m). The next three highest mountains are in Colorado: Mount Elbert, Mount Massive, and Mount Harvard.

Where is the lowest point in the United States?

The lowest point, at 282 feet (86 m) below sea level, is Bad Water, in Death Valley, California.

What is the longest river in the United States?

The Mississippi River is 2,340 miles (3,767 km) long, making it the longest in the United States. The Missouri River, at 2,315 miles (3,727 km) long, is the second longest, and together they form the fourth longest river system in the world. The Missouri River begins its journey in the Rocky Mountains of southwestern Montana, and it joins the Mississippi River a few miles north of St. Louis, Missouri.

Why does California have so many earthquakes?

Because the San Andreas fault runs though some 800 miles of the state. The San Andreas fault is a fracture in the earth's crust. Geologists call it a strike-slip type of fault, meaning the rock on one side of the fault moves sideways in relation to the rock on the other side. This movement causes earthquakes.

The San Andreas fault marks the place where two of the world's major tectonic plates—the North American and the Northern Pacific—meet. The Northern Pacific

Earthquakes in Missouri

The West Coast of the United States isn't the only place where major earthquakes can occur. Geologists predict that there is a 90 percent probability that the New Madrid fault in southeastern Missouri will produce a magnitude 6 or 7 earthquake within the next 50 years. Millions of people living in the Mississippi Valley area, including those in Memphis, Tennessee, and St. Louis, Missouri, would be affected.

plate is moving northwestward past the North American plate at a rate of about 2 inches (5 cm) per year.

What was the most powerful earthquake to ever occur in the United States?

Alaska's Good Friday earthquake in 1964 in Prince William Sound measured 9.2 on the Richter scale, the strongest ever recorded in the United States. This quake was felt over a 500,000-square-mile (1,295,000 sq km) area, killed 114 people, and released more than 125 times the energy of the San Francisco earthquake of 1906.

The San Francisco earthquake was the most destructive, however. It claimed 700 lives and caused millions of dollars in damage, much of it resulting from the fires that followed. Scientists at the U.S. Geological Survey estimate that it had a magnitude of 7.7.

Which countries does the United States trade with the most?

Not surprisingly, the United States conducts most of its trade with its two neighbors, Canada and Mexico. It also trades heavily with Japan, Germany, South Korea, Taiwan, and Great Britain.

What is NAFTA?

It's the North American Free Trade Agreement, which was signed by the United States, Canada, and Mexico in 1994. It means that these countries can trade freely with one another without having to pay taxes or duties on the goods traded.

What kinds of products does the United States sell to other countries?

Machinery and transportation equipment, especially airplanes, computers, and cars and trucks, top the list. Also important are manufactured items, metal, paper, textile fibers, metal ores, chemicals, and plastics.

Even though about one-third of the food exported in the world comes from U.S. farms, agriculture is not a large part of U.S. trade with other countries.

What types of products does the United States buy from other countries?

The United States imports thousands of different products from other countries, but leading the list, in order, are oil and gas; cars, trucks, and other motor vehicles; electrical machinery and appliances; telecommunications equipment; computers and office machines; toys and sporting goods; and clothing and clothing accessories.

Is Puerto Rico part of the United States?

Yes. Puerto Rico, an island in the Caribbean southeast of Florida, is a U.S. territory with 3.8 million people. Puerto Rico became a U.S. territory, along with the Pacific island of Guam, when the Treaty of Paris was signed after the Spanish-American War in 1898. Puerto Rico became a commonwealth in 1952, meaning that it governs itself under its own constitution.

Are the Virgin Islands also part of the United States?

Yes, the U.S. Virgin Islands (not to be confused with the British Virgin Islands) are a territory of the United States. They lie about 40 miles east of Puerto Rico. Because the U.S. government wanted to control this strategic spot in the Caribbean during World War I, it purchased this group of 50 islands and cays from Denmark in 1917.

How many people move from other countries to live in the United States each year?

Almost 1 million people immigrate to the United States yearly, although the Census Bureau predicts that the number will drop to about 700,000 a year by 2010. The main reason people come to the United States is for better-paying jobs. For example, one study noted that people who were earning about $31 a week in Mexico could make $278 a week in the United States.

How many people living in the United States don't speak English as their first language?

More than 30 million Americans are non-native speakers of English. Spanish-speaking people lead the list, followed by native speakers of French, German, Italian, Chinese, Tagalog, Polish, Korean, and Vietnamese.

What were the 10 largest metropolitan areas in population in the United States in 2000?

1.	New York, New York	21.1 million
2.	Los Angeles, California	16.3 million
3.	Chicago, Illinois	9.1 million
4.	Washington, D.C.	7.6 million
5.	San Francisco, California	7.0 million
6.	Philadelphia, Pennsylvania	6.1 million
7.	Boston, Massachusetts	5.8 million
8.	Detroit, Michigan	5.4 million
9.	Dallas–Fort Worth, Texas	5.2 million
10.	Houston, Texas	4.6 million

Almost half the world's people earn their living on farms or in farm-related activities. But in the United States, fewer than 3 people out of 100 work on farms.

Which are the leading U.S. farm states?

California leads the country in agricultural production, followed in order by Texas, Iowa, Kansas, and Nebraska.

North Dakota produces the most wheat, followed by Kansas. Iowa produces the most corn, followed by Illinois

THE UNITED STATES OF AMERICA AND ITS MAJOR CITIES

ALASKA

CANADA

Hudson Bay

49th parallel

WASHINGTON
Seattle
Portland
OREGON
IDAHO
MONTANA
NORTH DAKOTA
SOUTH DAKOTA
WYOMING
MINNESOTA
WISCONSIN
MICHIGAN
Detroit
NEBRASKA
IOWA
Chicago
OHIO
INDIANA
WEST VIRGINIA
MAINE
VERMONT
NEW HAMPSHIRE
MASSACHUSSETTS
NEW YORK
New York
RHODE ISLAND
CONNECTICUT
PENNSYLVANIA
NEW JERSEY
Washington D.C.
DELAWARE
MARYLAND
VIRGINIA

UNITED STATES OF AMERICA

NEVADA
San Francisco
CALIFORNIA
Los Angeles
UTAH
Denver
COLORADO
ARIZONA
NEW MEXICO
KANSAS
OKLAHOMA
TEXAS
Dallas
Houston
MISSOURI
ILLINOIS
KENTUCKY
TENNESSEE
ARKANSAS
MISSISSIPPI
LOUISIANA
New Orleans
ALABAMA
NORTH CAROLINA
SOUTH CAROLINA
GEORGIA
FLORIDA
Miami

ATLANTIC OCEAN

HAWAII

MEXICO

Gulf of Mexico

PACIFIC OCEAN

1000 miles
1000 km

and Nebraska. Texas produces the most cotton, followed by California and Mississippi.

Texas produces the most cattle, followed by Kansas and Nebraska. Iowa leads the states in hog production, followed by North Carolina. Arkansas is tops in poultry production.

The United States dominates North America. Its 50 states include 48 contiguous states (states sharing at least one border) and Alaska and Hawaii.

Did Texas ever belong to Mexico?

Yes, but when U.S. citizens began settling there in the early 1800s, they revolted because they didn't like the Mexican government's efforts to control them. In 1836, at the Battle of San Jacinto, near today's Houston, the American settlers captured Mexican general Santa Anna, who agreed to give Texas its independence.

In those days, Texas also included parts of today's Colorado, Kansas, New Mexico, Oklahoma, and Wyoming.

Weren't California, Arizona, New Mexico, and some other U.S. states also once part of Mexico?

Yes. At the end of the Mexican War in 1848, Mexico gave the United States the land that is now California, Nevada, and Utah. It also turned over most of Arizona and parts of Colorado, New Mexico, and Wyoming.

In the Gadsden Purchase of 1853, Mexico sold the land that now forms southern Arizona and New Mexico to the United States for $10 million.

Mexico is the largest Spanish-speaking country in the world.

Is Mexico City larger than New York City?

No. In 2000 the New York City metropolitan area was slightly larger, with 21.1 million people. Mexico City had 18.1 million people in its metropolitan area and is ranked the fourth largest city in the world, after Tokyo, Japan; New York City; and Seoul-Inchon, South Korea. (See the list of the world's 10 largest cities on page 25.)

Does Mexico have states, like the United States?

Yes, it has 31 states and a federal district, Mexico City, which is the capital.

Is Mexico mostly dry and desertlike?

About 70 percent of Mexico is arid or semiarid, but the country also has beautiful mountain ranges, scenic beaches, and lush tropical forests.

What is the highest mountain in Mexico?

The highest point in Mexico is Pico de Orizaba (Citlaltepetl), which rises 18,410 feet (5,610 m) above sea level. It's about 65 miles west of Veracruz.

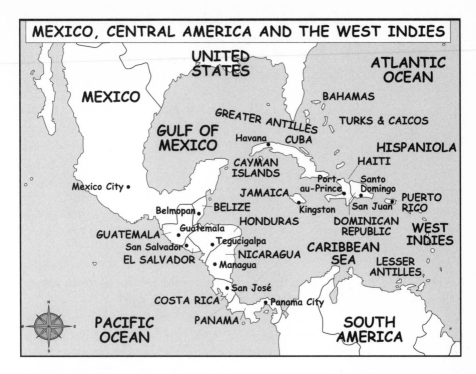

MEXICO, CENTRAL AMERICA AND THE WEST INDIES

UNITED STATES
ATLANTIC OCEAN
MEXICO
BAHAMAS
GREATER ANTILLES
TURKS & CAICOS
GULF OF MEXICO
Havana   CUBA
HISPANIOLA
CAYMAN ISLANDS
HAITI
Mexico City •
Port-au-Prince
Santo Domingo
JAMAICA
PUERTO RICO
Belmopan • BELIZE
Kingston
San Juan
HONDURAS
GUATEMALA   Guatemala
DOMINICAN REPUBLIC
WEST INDIES
San Salvador •   • Tegucigalpa
CARIBBEAN SEA
EL SALVADOR   • Managua
NICARAGUA
LESSER ANTILLES
• San José
COSTA RICA
• Panama City
PACIFIC OCEAN
PANAMA
SOUTH AMERICA

What is Mexico's largest lake?

Lake Chapala, in the state of Jalisco, covers 651 square miles (1,686 sq km).

What's the name of the active volcano south of Mexico City?

Popocatepetl, which is one of the tallest mountains in North America at 17,887 feet (54,520 m). It's been erupting since at least the 1300s, and most recently in 2000. Its name is an Aztec word meaning "smoking mountain."

Why does Mexico have so many earthquakes and volcanoes?

Mexico sits on top of not one or two but three of the earth's tectonic plates. For this reason, the country experiences more than its share of earthquakes, since the movement of these plates causes earthquakes and volcanoes. One of the worst earthquakes to hit the country killed thousands of people and caused the destruction of more than 6,000 buildings in Mexico City in 1985. It measured 8.1 on the Richter scale.

Mexico, Central America, and the West Indies are home to numerous different languages and cultures. Many countries are former colonies of Great Britain, France, Spain, or Holland.

Are the people who live in Mexico of Spanish or Indian descent?

Most of today's Mexicans are descendants of *both* Indian and Spanish people, a combination called mestizo. For nearly 300 years, between 1521 and 1810, people from Spain ruled Mexico, claiming it as a colony. But for thousands of years previously, various Indian empires, including the Aztecs and the Maya, built advanced civilizations there.

About 60 percent of the Mexican people today are considered to be mestizo, while 30 percent are Indian. About one in six Indians primarily speaks an Indian language, such as Maya, Mixtec, Nahuatl, Otomi, Tarascan, or Zapotec.

Is it true that a giant asteroid hit the earth in what is now Mexico millions of years ago?

Yes, scientists believe that an asteroid measuring about 6 miles (10 km) wide slammed into what is now the village of Chicxulub in Mexico's Yucatan Peninsula about 65 million years ago. The impact created a crater 124 miles (200 km) in diameter and threw billions of tons of vaporized rock, water, and gas into the atmosphere.

The asteroid's impact affected the entire world. It ignited firestorms and caused tidal waves, earthquakes, and hurricanes. The enormous amount of dust in the atmosphere blocked sunlight and made it impossible for many plants to grow and for many animals—who ate those plants—to survive. Scientists believe that more than half the plants and animals living on the earth at that time, including the dinosaurs, eventually became extinct as a result of the asteroid's impact.

What are maquiladoras?

They are manufacturing plants that assemble parts made elsewhere to produce items such as electronic equipment, clothes, auto parts, and appliances. They are located in northern Mexico, mostly within a few miles of the U.S. border. About 1 million Mexicans work in about 3,800 maquiladoras, which are owned primarily by U.S., Japanese, and European companies.

Most of the workers are young women between the ages of 14 and 20 who are generally paid less than $2 an hour to work 10-hour days, 5 or 6 days a week. These plants take advantage of cheap labor costs in Mexico and easy access to U.S. trade routes.

Why does Mexico City suffer from so much air pollution?

Mexico City is one of the world's largest and fastest-growing cities, with more than 3 million cars and trucks and hundreds of industrial plants throwing pollutants into the air. Half of Mexico's industrial plants are located in or near Mexico City.

Geography has made air pollution problems even worse. Mexico City is located in a valley with mountains on three sides, which trap the bad air.

What ancient city was originally built on the site of today's Mexico City?

The Aztec capital of Tenochtitlan may have had as many as 400,000 residents when the Spanish explorers first saw it in 1519. It was one of the world's largest cities at the time. The city was founded in 1325 on two large islands in the middle of Lake Texcoco. The Spaniards destroyed the city in 1521, but it was later rebuilt.

How big is Mexico compared with the United States?

In land area, Mexico is about three times the size of Texas. It is about one-fifth the size of the United States. In population, Mexico has 99 million people, while the United States has about 281 million people.

Which countries make up Central America?

Belize, Costa Rica, El Salvador, Guatemala, Honduras, Nicaragua, and Panama. About 37 million people live in those seven countries south of Mexico.

Are all of the people in Central American countries descended from the early Spanish settlers?

No, several different European and native groups are represented. But Spanish is the official language in all countries except Belize, which is English speaking.

Belize has the second-longest coral barrier reef in the world, after Australia's Great Barrier Reef.

El Salvador, like much of Central America, lies in a geologically active region. Its capital, San Salvador, has been laid to ruin at least 10 times in the past 400 years by earth-quakes.

Why was the Panama Canal built?

Because it provided a much-needed shortcut for ships to travel between the Atlantic and Pacific Oceans. Before the canal was built, ships had to sail around the southern tip of South America, taking them thousands of miles out of their way through dangerous waters.

In which directions do ships go when they pass through the Panama Canal?

Ships travel north and south through the Panama Canal, not east and west. A look at a map of the isthmus of Panama makes it clear why.

How long did it take to build the Panama Canal?

About 10 years, from 1904 until 1914. It cuts through the isthmus of Panama for about 51 miles (82 km) from Limon Bay on the Atlantic Ocean to the Bay of Panama on the Pacific Ocean.

From 1903 until 1979, a 10-mile-wide strip of land called the Panama Canal Zone was controlled by the United States, which built the canal. The United States continued to operate the canal for another 20 years, until 1999, when it was turned over to the government of Panama.

The Panama Canal connects the Caribbean and the North Pacific Ocean, making it possible for ships to go from the Atlantic to the Pacific without rounding the southern tip of South America.

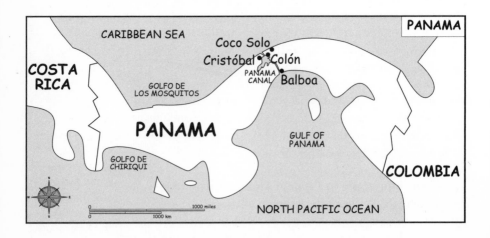

Is there a highway that runs from North America through Central America and into South America?

No, because there is a 54-mile- (87-km) long gap in the Pan-American Highway, a system of roads connecting countries in North and South America. This missing section prevents traffic from passing through the isthmus of Panama into the South American country of Colombia.

Back in the 1960s, work began to complete the highway through the Panamanian province of Darién. But construction was stopped about halfway through because people became concerned that opening the border between Panama and Colombia might expose countries in Central and North America to foot-and-mouth disease, a serious problem in South America's cattle industry at the time.

The Building of the Panama Canal

Since the 1500s sailors had longed for a shortcut between the Atlantic and Pacific Oceans. Finally, in 1881, a French company made the first attempt at digging a canal through the isthmus of Panama, the narrowest stretch of land in Central America. But the project was abandoned seven years later, after little progress had been made and 20,000 workers had died from accidents and disease (primarily yellow fever and malaria).

In 1902, U.S. president Theodore Roosevelt pushed through a plan that bought rights from the French company and negotiated a treaty with Panama. Construction resumed under U.S. management in 1904, and the canal was opened in 1914. Between 1881 and 1914, an esti-mated 80,000 people worked on the canal. It was one of the most ambitious and difficult engineering projects in history.

Yellow fever and malaria remained a problem at first, until U.S. Army doctor William Gorgas was brought in to help eliminate the diseases. His colleague in Cuba, Dr. Walter Reed, had earlier discovered that the diseases were spread by mosquitoes.

It takes a ship about eight to ten hours to make the trip through the canal. By using the canal instead of going around South America, a ship traveling from New York to San Francisco can shave nearly 8,000 miles (12,880 km) off its journey. About 14,000 ships travel through the canal each year.

If the road is ever completed, it will be possible to drive the 16,000 miles (25,760 km) from Alaska to the bottom of Chile. Plans to complete the road are once again being discussed, but today many people are opposed to the project because the road would cut through hundreds of acres of biologically diverse rain forest in Panama and Colombia.

El Salvador is the only Central American country that does not have a Caribbean coastline.

Why has Costa Rica become such a popular tourist destination?

Costa Rica's government has been working to promote the country as a prime ecotourism destination. It has more than 850 species of birds, 1,400 species of trees, 9,000 flowering plants, at least 4,500 different types of moths, and many other exotic forms of wildlife. Almost one-third of the country's land is protected by the government.

Which islands make up the West Indies, in the Caribbean Sea?

The 2,000-mile-long island chain known as the West Indies is divided into three groups of islands. Their total population is about the same as that of Central America—about 37 million. In the following list, islands that are followed by a country name in parentheses are territories of that country; the others are independent nations.

First, starting at the northern end, are the Bahamas, consisting of about 3,000 small islands southeast of Florida. The Turks and Caicos (United Kingdom) are an island group south of the Bahamas.

Next are the Greater Antilles, near the center of the West Indies; they include Cuba, Jamaica, Hispaniola (which contains the countries of Haiti and the Dominican Republic), and Puerto Rico (United States). The Cayman Islands (United Kingdom) lie south of Cuba.

Jamaica is one of the world's leading exporters of alumina, a mineral derived from bauxite ore that is used to make aluminum.

The third group is the Lesser Antilles, starting east of Puerto Rico and curving south toward Venezuela in South America. They include, roughly from north to south, St. Thomas, St. John, and St. Croix (United States); Tortola, Virgin Gorda, and Anegada (United Kingdom); Anguilla (United Kingdom), St. Martin/St. Maarten (France and the

Netherlands), St. Barthelemy (France), Saba and St. Eustatius (the Netherlands), St. Kitts and Nevis, Antigua and Barbuda, Montserrat (United Kingdom), Guadeloupe (France), Dominica, Martinique (France), St. Lucia, Barbados, St. Vincent and the Grenadines, Grenada, and Trinidad and Tobago.

Curving back westward above the coast of Venezuela, the Lesser Antilles continue with Bonaire, Curaçao, and Aruba (Netherlands).

Is it true that the land that Christopher Columbus first sighted in October 1492 was really an island in the West Indies?

Yes—Columbus never saw the North American mainland. The land he first saw was an island in the Bahamas, which he named San Salvador.

Columbus called this region the Indies because he thought he had reached the islands we now call the East Indies in Asia.

Why did so many European countries colonize the West Indies?

Back in the 1700s and 1800s, sugar cane was a profitable crop that was easily grown on these islands. People from Spain, the United Kingdom, France, and the Netherlands first forced native people to work for them, then later brought slave labor from Africa to work on the large plantations they built there.

Is the volcano on Montserrat still active?

Yes, and geologists will be keeping a close eye on volcanic activity on this small island for years to come. Montserrat's Soufriere Hills volcano began erupting in 1995 and will probably continue to pose a danger to island residents for at least another 10 years.

What makes Boiling Lake on the island of Dominica boil?

Geologists think that Boiling Lake is actually a flooded fumarole, which is a crack in the earth's surface

Grenada is the world's top producer of nutmeg, a spice that comes from the nutmeg tree's seeds. Nutmeg trees were brought to Grenada from the Moluccas, also known as the Spice Islands, in Indonesia.

that releases gases from molten lava below. These gases bubble to the surface, making it look as if the lake is boiling. The water itself is almost hot enough to boil, at 197°F (92°C). The lake is 207 feet (63 m) wide and is usually topped with a cloud of steam.

CHAPTER 3

SOUTH AMERICA

How many countries make up South America?

Twelve. From largest to smallest in population, the countries are Brazil, Colombia, Argentina, Peru, Venezuela, Chile, Ecuador, Bolivia, Paraguay, Uruguay, Guyana, and Suriname. French Guiana belongs to France, and the Falkland Islands, the island of South Georgia, and the South Sandwich Islands are territories of the United Kingdom.

How large is Brazil?

Brazil is so large that it includes about half of South America's population and occupies half of the continent's land area. It's the fifth largest country in the world, both in land area and in population. It's about the same size as the contiguous 48 United States in land area.

Do more people live in North America than in South America?

Yes. About 345 million people lived in South America in 2000. North America's population (including Central America and the Caribbean) was more than 408 million people.

All of South America lies east of the North American city of Savannah, Georgia.

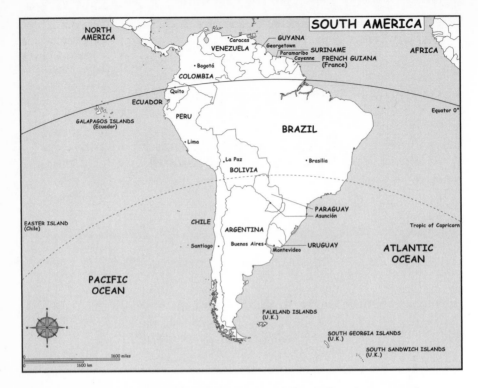

Brazil is by far the largest of the 12 countries that make up South America.

South America, the fourth largest continent, is home to 6 percent of the world's population and accounts for 12 percent of its land area. The tropical rain forest in the Amazon River Basin is the largest in the world.

Is Spanish the most widely spoken language in South America?

No, nearly half the people speak Portuguese—most of them in Brazil—although Spanish isn't far behind. Portuguese is the official language of Brazil, which was founded as a Portuguese territory in 1494.

Three other languages are widely spoken in South America. In Peru, Bolivia, Argentina, and Ecuador, 8 million people speak Quechua. In Paraguay, 4 million people speak Tup (also called Guarani). In Bolivia and Peru, 2 million people speak Aymara.

Is South America the same as Latin America?

No, Latin America refers more to culture than geography. Latin America usually means South America as well as Mexico, Central America, and the Caribbean, which are geographically part of North America. Many of these countries were settled by Spanish, Portuguese, and French colonists. All of those groups speak languages that evolved from Latin—thus the term Latin America.

Where do the Andes mountains begin and end?

The snow-covered peaks of the Andes stretch along the west coast of South America for about 4,500 miles (7,200 km), running from Venezuela in the north to Tierra del Fuego in the south. They make up the longest mountain range above sea level in the world. Because the Andes are still forming as a result of tectonic forces, the region experiences frequent earthquakes and volcanoes. These mountains are rich in minerals, such as gold, copper, lead, and tin.

Are the Andes taller than the Himalayas in Asia?

No, they are not as high as the Himalayas, even though many peaks in the Andes are higher than 20,000 feet (6,100 m) above sea level. Peaks in the Himalayas reach more than 26,240 feet (8,000 m).

How big is the Amazon River?

The Amazon is the largest of the five river systems in South America. Its source is in the Andes mountains of Peru. From there it flows eastward for 4,000 miles (6,437 km) across Brazil and into the Atlantic Ocean. It is the second longest river in the world, after the Nile in Africa.

The Amazon carries much more water than the Nile, though—in fact, it accounts for one-fifth of the world's fresh river water. At one point near the Atlantic Ocean, the Amazon is 40 miles (64 km) wide.

What is the largest lake in South America?

Venezuela's Lake Maracaibo, which covers 5,217 square miles (13,512 sq km).

Where is the world's highest waterfall?

The world's highest waterfall is Angel Falls, in eastern Venezuela, with a drop of 3,212 feet (979 m). South America's most beautiful waterfall is Iguazú Falls, on the border of Argentina and Brazil. These falls are the result of the Iguazú River dropping 237 feet (72 m) over a cliff that is nearly 2 miles (3.2 km) wide.

Three out of every four people in South America live in cities.

Most of the world's coffee comes from Brazil and Colombia.

Lake Titicaca, on the border of Peru and Bolivia, is the highest navigable lake in the world. Perched in the Andes, the lake's elevation is 12,507 feet (812 m).

Is South America mostly mountains and rain forest?

No, much of the continent is farmland and grazing lands. Scrubland runs through northeastern Brazil, and deserts are found in Ecuador, Peru, Patagonia, and even in the northern coastal areas of Chile, Colombia, and Venezuela. Arica, a port city in northern Chile, is one of the driest places on the planet—it receives only 0.03 inch (0.76 cm) of rain a year.

Only one glacier in the world is found at 0° latitude—that is, on the Equator. It's on Mount Cotopaxi in Ecuador.

What is the biggest threat to South America's forests?

Logging activites are the biggest destroyer of South American forests, but mining, energy exploration, and road building are also major threats.

What kinds of natural resources are found in South America?

South America is rich in natural resources of all kinds. Venezuela, Argentina, Brazil, Colombia, Ecuador, and Peru produce petroleum products. Brazil has tin, iron ore, and manganese mines. Tin is also mined in Bolivia. Bauxite, an ore used to make aluminum, comes from mines in Brazil, Guyana, and Suriname.

Chile is the world's top producer of copper and is the only country in the world with deposits of sodium nitrate, used to make fertilizer. Peru is known for its copper, lead, and zinc mines.

Most of the world's emeralds come from mines in Colombia, which also has rich deposits of coal. Fishing

Food from South America

Many of the food items that people all over the world enjoy originated in South America. For example, potatoes were first cultivated about 7,000 years ago in the Andes mountains. Tomatoes were also first grown in South America, in the area of today's Peru and Ecuador. Also native to the continent are peanuts, yams, pineapples, lima beans, and several types of peppers and chilies. If it weren't for a bean called cacao, also native to South America, we wouldn't have chocolate.

also helps to support the economies of Peru and Chile. Forest products are important to Brazil.

Even with all of this natural wealth, most people in South America are poor. Although the middle class is growing, the people with money are those who own factories, mines, and large farms and ranches. The richest country is Argentina, and the poorest is Guyana.

Col... Chil... only ...... American countries that touch both the Pacific and Atlantic oceans.

How did Venezuela get its name?

The Indians living in this area in the 1500s built their houses on stilts over the waters of Lake Maracaibo and elsewhere. These structures reminded an early Spanish explorer of the buildings and homes in Venice, which are perched over water. He called the land Venezuela, which means "little Venice" in Spanish.

Did Christopher Columbus ever set foot in North or South America?

The only time Christopher Columbus saw either of the American continents was in 1498, when he landed in what is now Venezuela.

Almost all the carnations and about one-third of the roses sold in the United States are grown in Colombia.

What makes the Galapagos Islands so special?

Located in the Pacific Ocean about 620 miles (1,000 km) off the western South American coast, the Galapagos Islands became famous after Charles Darwin published his *Origin of Species,* describing a theory of evolution, in 1859. His ideas were based in part on the unique animal species he observed on these isolated islands several years earlier.

The Galapagos consist of 13 large volcanic islands and 6 smaller ones. They are home to many unusual animals, including birds, turtles, iguanas, and penguins. Only about 15,000 people live there permanently, but about 60,000 people visit the islands each year from all over the world.

Which country do the Galapagos Islands belong to?

They are part of Ecuador, a small country in northwestern South America on the Equator between Colombia and Peru.

Ecuador's name comes from the Spanish word for "Equator."

Are most Peruvians of Spanish descent?

No. About one-half of the Peruvian people are Indians, and most of the rest are of mixed white and Indian ancestry. Peru is home to the highest percentage of Indians of any South American country. Their ancestors were the Incas, who created an advanced civilization in Peru between 1200 and 1500. In the 1520s, the Spanish conquered Peru, and it remained a Spanish colony for the next 300 years. About 800 people immigrated to Peru from Japan in the early 1900s to work as farm laborers. About 100,000 people of Japanese descent now live in Peru, including former Peruvian president Alberto Fujimori.

What language do people in Peru speak?

Peru has two official languages: Spanish and Quechua, the native Inca language. Most Peruvian people speak Spanish.

What makes the Inca ruins at Machu Picchu in Peru so unusual?

Archaeologists aren't sure why the Incas built this city with its terraced gardens so high (7,710 feet/2,350 m) in the Andes Mountains. But they have noted that it sits in a unique geographic location: on the days of the spring and fall equinoxes and the winter and summer solstices, the sun rises directly behind certain nearby mountains.

What's the difference between the two countries named Guiana and Guyana in South America?

Guyana, in northeastern South America, is an independent country, while French Guiana, a bit farther to the east on the continent, belongs to France. Guyana was a British possession until 1966, when its name was changed from British Guiana to Guyana.

French Guiana is one of the richest places on the continent, but that is largely because it is heavily supported by France. Until about 50 years ago, France sent convicts to penal colonies there.

Guyana is separated from French Guiana by the country of Suriname. Guyana is about the size of Utah. In

1595, Sir Walter Raleigh searched there for the legendary city of gold, El Dorado. Although it has many valuable mineral resources, the country has not been completely explored or developed. Today it is known for its sugar plantations and rice farms.

What is the smallest country in South America?

Suriname, on the continent's northeast coast, is the smallest in both land area and population. Most people live in the port city of Paramaribo. Suriname was a colony of the Netherlands until 1975.

Dutch is still the official language, but 10 other languages are spoken there, the most common of which is Sranan Tongo. In addition to native Indians, Suriname's people are of many different ethnic groups, including Indian, African, Indonesian, Chinese, and European.

How large is Brazil's rain forest?

The Amazonian rain forest in Brazil is the largest in the world. It's about five times the size of Texas. Human activities in the region—especially logging, farming, ranching, and road building—continue to destroy more acres of this rain forest every day. Between 1980 and 1990, Brazil lost about 5.4 million acres (2.16 hectares) of rain forest, an area larger than New Jersey.

Because the earth's crust below Brazil is very ancient and stable, the country has never had an earthquake or a volcanic eruption.

Why are rain forests important?

Tropical rain forests play a major role in sustaining all the earth's living things, both plants and animals. Trees take in carbon dioxide and produce oxygen. Fewer trees mean that more carbon dioxide remains in the atmosphere, which contributes to global warming as well as to destruction of places for plants and animals to live. Also, with fewer trees, less moisture evaporates into the atmosphere, meaning that less rain may fall in the surrounding region.

Tropical rain forests contain about half the plant and animal species in the world. If these species lose their habitats, they will begin to die off, and some species may disappear forever.

Brazil borders every other South American country but two: Peru and Chile.

The city of São Paulo, Brazil, is the fifth largest city in the world, with nearly 18 million people.

In Brazil, about 10 million children and young people live on the streets. About one of every three children between the ages of 5 and 17 who live in the countryside have jobs.

Why did Brazil move its capital from Rio de Janeiro to the new city of Brasília?

After World War II, the large coastal city of Rio de Janeiro became so crowded and inefficient that the government decided to create a new capital city farther inland. They also wanted to encourage people to move to the central part of the country, away from the heavily populated coastal areas. Brasília was built from the ground up, and it became Brazil's capital in 1960.

Do all South American countries touch the ocean?

No, Bolivia and Paraguay are landlocked, meaning they have no access to the sea. At one time, part of Bolivia did reach the Pacific, but it lost that land to Chile in a war.

Where are the highest and lowest points in South America?

Both extremes are in Argentina. Mount Aconcagua in the Andes, the highest point in the Western Hemisphere, is 22,834 feet (6,960 m) high, while Salinas Chicas on the Valdes Peninsula in eastern Argentina is 131 feet (40 m) below sea level.

Who are the Portenos?

Portenos—meaning "people of the port"—are citizens of Argentina's capital and largest city, Buenos Aires. They represent people of various cultures, including Italian, German, and Spanish. Buenos Aires is considered to be the most European city in South America.

Is Patagonia a country?

No. Patagonia is the name of a region that covers the southern part of Argentina. It is a semiarid plateau, and farmers raise sheep there. It also has important resources, including oil fields and coal and iron ore deposits.

What famous person is Bolivia named after?

The country is named after the Venezuelan general Simon Bolivar, who helped the former Spanish colony

The Atacama Desert

Chile's Atacama Desert is the second driest region in the world, after Antarctica. No plants grow there. Its elevation is about 8,000 feet (2,438 m), with average temperatures ranging from 32° to 75°F (0° to 25°C). It rains there about once every 100 years. This is due to its location on the eastern side of the Coast Range, which results in a weather phenomenon known as the rain shadow effect. When moist air from the ocean rises up the western side of these mountains, it cools and the water condenses, producing rain. But when the air goes down the eastern side of the mountains, it grows warmer and drier.

The Atacama receives some precipitation in the form of fog in the coastal areas and of snow in the mountains.

Much of Chile's copper comes from mines in the Atacama Desert.

gain its independence in 1825. Simon Bolivar is considered to be a great liberator in South America, and he inspired many leaders to fight to free the continent from Spanish control.

How did Argentina get its name?

Argentina's name comes from the Latin word for "silver," *argentum*. That's the precious metal that attracted Spanish settlers there in the 1500s. They didn't find silver, but they found fertile soils that brought the citizens riches from the production of grains and cattle centuries later.

The southernmost town in the world is in Argentina: Ushuaia, in Tierra del Fuego.

How wide is Chile?

Chile is only 265 miles (427 km) wide at its widest point. The country, on the Pacific coast of South America, is more than 10 times as long as it is wide. Its southern tip is Tierra del Fuego, an archipelago (a large group of islands) south of the Strait of Magellan that it shares with Argentina.

Who built the giant stone statues on Easter Island?

Easter Island is a small volcanic island of about 64 square miles (166 sq km) in the South Pacific Ocean. It is

The giant stone moai of Easter Island range in height from 13 to 20 feet. The culture and people who created them 16 centuries ago remain a mystery.

about 2,300 miles (3,700 km) west of Chile and 2,000 miles (3,220 km) east of Tahiti, making it one of the most isolated places in the world.

Easter Island belongs to Chile, and nearly 3,000 people live there today. No one knows for sure who erected the 600 stone statues, called *moai,* more than 1,600 years ago. They may have been people from Polynesia, or they may have been South American Indians.

Easter Island was named by a Dutch sea captain who discovered it on Easter Sunday in 1722.

Why is Europe considered a continent? ◆ What is the
longest river in Europe? What is the highest mountain in
Europe? ◆ Where is Europe's largest lake? ◆ How did the
Black Sea get its name? ◆ Why does most of western
Europe have such a mild climate even though it lies so far
north? ◆ How many countries are there in Europe? ◆ Why
is Europe's popul   European country has the largest population? What is the most widely
practiced religion in Europe? ◆ What is the European
Union? ◆ How many different languages are spoken in
Europe? ◆ What is a euro? ◆ Why was the euro introduced? ◆ What is the longest tunnel in Europe? ◆ Why is I

CHAPTER 4

EUROPE

Why is Europe considered a continent?

Because Europe is a principal division of land, which is how geographers have traditionally defined a continent. In reality, Europe is part of one huge landmass known as Eurasia. But because the cultures of Asia and Europe are so different, geographers have historically considered Europe a separate continent.

Europe is bordered on the west by the Atlantic Ocean and on the east by the Ural Mountains, the Ural River, and the Caspian Sea.

Thousands of islands, including Iceland, Great Britain, and Ireland, are also considered part of Europe.

What is the longest river in Europe?

The Volga River, which flows entirely within Russia, is Europe's longest. From its source in the hills northwest of Moscow, the Volga travels almost 2,300 miles (3,700 km) to the Caspian Sea. Much of Russia's freight is carried on barges on this river. The Volga's waters supply irrigation for the wheat farms along its banks and also power several hydroelectric plants.

The Danube River is Europe's second longest, at almost 1,770 miles (2,860 km). The Danube passes through Austria, Slovakia, Hungary, Yugoslavia, Bulgaria, and Romania before it empties into the Black Sea.

The Danube River flows through more countries than any other river in the world.

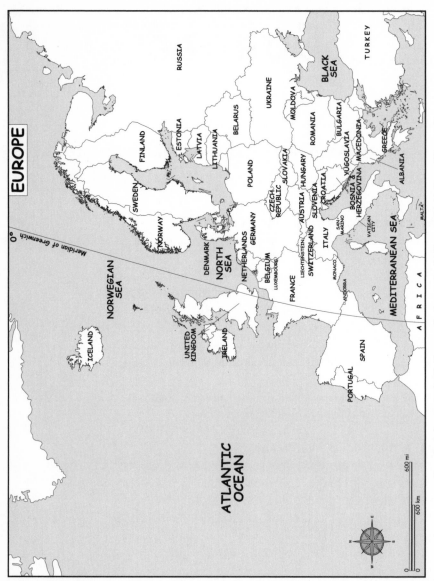

Europe is home to both the smallest country in the world, Vatican City, and the largest, Russia. However, much of the landmass of Russia lies in Asia.

What is the highest mountain in Europe?

Mount Elbrus, in the Caucasus Mountains in south-western Russia, is the tallest peak in Europe, at 18,510 feet (5,642 m).

The Alps are Europe's largest mountain chain. They extend for about 660 miles (1,060 km) across south-central Europe. The tallest mountain in the Alps is Mont Blanc, at 15,771 feet (4,807 km), on the border of France, Italy, and Switzerland.

Where is Europe's largest lake?

The world's largest lake—the Caspian Sea—is partly in Europe and partly in Asia. It's a lake, not a sea, because it is completely surrounded by land. The Caspian is about 750 miles long (1,210 km) and 300 miles (483 km) wide at its widest point.

Finland has the most lakes of any country in Europe—about 60,000.

The Caspian contains salt water, not freshwater. The water is salty because the lake is losing more water through evaporation than it receives from the streams that flow into it. When freshwater evaporates, salt sediments are left behind.

The Caspian is growing smaller every year. Its north-western shore is the lowest point in Europe, at 92 feet (28 m) below sea level.

Europe's largest freshwater lake is Ladoga, in north-western Russia.

How did the Black Sea get its name?

The Black Sea, which touches the countries of Ukraine, Russia, Georgia, Turkey, Bulgaria, and Romania, apparently got its name because heavy winter fog and storms make the sea look black. The Black Sea is larger than the state of California, covering about 173,000 square miles (448,000 sq km). Ships can travel between the Black Sea and the Mediterranean Sea through the Bosporus Strait, the Sea of Marmara, and the Dardanelles Strait.

Why does most of western Europe have such a mild climate even though it lies so far north?

The winds that blow from the west into Europe are warmed by the Gulf Stream, which is a strong Atlantic

Ocean current that brings warm water from the regions near the Equator north to Europe's western coasts. Even Norway's coast, part of which lies within the frigid Arctic Circle, is not bothered by snow and ice during the winter months because of the warming effects of the Gulf Stream.

How many countries are there in Europe?

Europe has 47 independent countries of all sizes, from the largest in the world (in land area)—Russia—to the smallest—Vatican City. About one of every eight people in the world lives in Europe. However, the population of Europe is slowly declining, while most of the rest of the world is growing. In 2000, there were 703 million people living in Europe.

In the 1950s, Europeans made up 22 percent of the world population, but by 2000 their percentage had dropped to 12 percent.

Why is Europe's population shrinking?

During the late 1990s, more people were dying in Europe than were being born. Women there are having fewer children than in any other part of the world. The only European country where women are having enough children to keep the population at the same level is Albania.

Women in Bulgaria and the Czech Republic are having, on average, just 1.1 children these days. Other countries with very low birth rates are Russia, Italy, Slovenia, Estonia, Spain, and Latvia.

Which European country has the largest population?

Russia is the largest, with 146 million people (that's about half as many people as in the United States). The next largest countries, in order, are Germany, France, the United Kingdom, Italy, and Ukraine.

What is the most widely practiced religion in Europe?

Christianity, by far. More than half of European Christians are Roman Catholic; the rest are Eastern Orthodox, Protestant, or Anglican.

What is the European Union?

The European Union—the EU for short—is made up of 15 western European countries that cooperate on certain political matters and that are working together to form a united European economy. The EU members are Austria, Belgium, Denmark, Finland, France, Germany, Greece, Ireland, Italy, Luxembourg, the Netherlands, Portugal, Spain, Sweden, and the United Kingdom.

How many different languages are spoken in Europe?

People in the 47 European countries speak about 50 languages and more than 100 dialects, which are the regional variations of a language. Within the 15 countries of the European Union, the most widely spoken language is English. About 16 percent speak English as a first language and another 31 percent speak it well enough to hold a conversation. The next most widely spoken languages are German and French. Almost half the people in the European Union countries can speak a language other than their mother tongue.

What is a euro?

The euro is a new form of official currency in 12 European countries: Austria, Belgium, Finland, France, Germany, Greece, Ireland, Italy, Luxembourg, the Netherlands, Portugal, and Spain. In 2002, these countries began using euro bills and coins instead of their own currencies. The three remaining European Union countries—Denmark, Sweden, and Great Britain—still use their own forms of money, but they may switch to the euro someday.

European leaders hope that a single currency will strengthen Europe's position as a world economic power.

Why was the euro introduced?

The euro makes it easy to conduct business with other EU member countries and among world nations. For example, travelers visiting EU countries no longer have

Agriculture is big business in Europe, where more than half the land is used for farming. Wheat is the biggest crop.

to carry different national currencies for each country they visit.

About one-fourth of all the railroad track in the world is in Europe.

What is the longest tunnel in Europe?

For many years, Europe's—and the world's—longest road tunnel was the 10.5-mile (16.9-km) St. Gotthard road tunnel in central Switzerland. But in 2000, Norway opened the 15.3-mile (24.5-km) Laerdal road tunnel that cuts through mountains to connect the capital, Oslo, with the port city of Bergen.

Switzerland is now building what will become the world's longest rail tunnel in the world, also through the Gotthard mountains. It will be 36 miles (58 km) long and will be completed in 2012.

Why is Iceland called the Land of Ice and Fire?

Iceland's parliament, the Althing, is the oldest unicameral (one-house) legislature in the world. It has been meeting since A.D. 930.

Because the island is full of glaciers, volcanoes, and hot springs. Iceland has more hot springs than any other country in the world. The English word *geyser* comes from the name for Iceland's most famous hot spring, Geysir. Glaciers cover almost one-eighth of the country.

Norway controlled Iceland from 1262 to 1380, when Denmark took over. Since 1944, Iceland has been an independent country.

Family Names in Iceland

Icelanders are unusual in that they do not have family names, like Smith and Jones. To come up with a distinctive name, boys add their first name to a second name that is a combination of their father's first name with the letters "son" added on the end. Girls combine their first names with their father's first name with the letters "dottir" added on the end. For example, if a man named Einar Johannson has a son named Petur, the son's full name is Petur Einarsson. If he has a daughter named Margret, her full name is Margret Einarsdottir. They can get by with this scheme because there aren't that many Icelanders. Still, many people do have the same name, so to help prevent confusion phone books in Iceland also list each person's occupation.

Do people in Iceland speak Danish?

No, they speak their own Scandinavian language called Icelandic. It's one of the most unchanged languages in the world, thanks to Iceland's geographic isolation. It is similar to Old Norse, which was spoken by the original settlers. Most people also speak English, German, or another Scandinavian language.

Is Scandinavia a country or a region?

Scandinavia is a region that comprises the countries of Norway, Sweden, and Denmark. Finland and Iceland are sometimes considered part of Scandinavia.

Why is Norway called the Land of the Midnight Sun?

The northern part of Norway is located above the Arctic Circle, where the sun shines 24 hours a day from mid-May to mid-July. In the winter months, the reverse happens, and the sun does not appear even during the daytime.

Is the United Kingdom the same thing as Great Britain?

Almost. Great Britain refers to the island that contains England, Wales, and Scotland; it's the eighth largest island in the world. The United Kingdom is the short name of the country that includes those three regions, plus Northern Ireland—the northeastern corner of the island of Ireland. The country's official name is the United Kingdom of Great Britain and Northern Ireland.

How much of the world did the the United Kingdom once rule?

In 1900, the United Kingdom ruled an empire that covered one-fourth of the world's land area. The empire slowly broke up, the result of two devastating world wars and the desire of most of the British colonies to gain independence.

What's the difference between Ireland and Northern Ireland?

Ireland has been home to the Republic of Ireland, an independent country, since 1921, when it broke away

THE U.K. AND IRELAND

Shetland
Islands

SCOTLAND

UNITED
KINGDOM

Glasgow

Edinburgh

IRELAND

NORTHERN
IRELAND

Belfast•

Dublin•

Liverpool

ENGLAND

•Birmingham

WALES

London•

150 miles

150 km

The United King-
dom of Great Britain
and Northern
Ireland includes
Scotland and Wales.
Ireland is a separate
country.

from the United Kingdom. It occupies about 83 percent of
the whole island, which is about the size of West Virginia,
while Northern Ireland, which is part of the United
Kingdom, takes up the rest.

Most people in Northern Ireland are Protestant, while
most in Ireland are Roman Catholic. Most people in

Ireland would like to see Northern Ireland returned to the Republic of Ireland, but most people in Northern Ireland wish to remain part of the United Kingdom. Violence and fighting over the idea of reunification along religious lines have been going on for many years.

Does everyone in the United Kingdom speak English?

Just about everyone. But several thousand people in Scotland also speak Scottish Gaelic, and some people in Northern Ireland speak Irish Gaelic. About one in five people in Wales speaks both Welsh and English, and a handful speak only Welsh. Welsh and Gaelic developed from the ancient Celtic language, which was spoken by the people who lived in Britain more than a thousand years ago.

Other Celtic languages are Manx, Cornish, and Breton. Manx and Cornish have died out—the last native speaker of Manx died in 1974—but attempts are being made to revive them. Manx was the only language spoken on the Isle of Man until the 1700s. Cornish was spoken until the early 1800s in Cornwall, which was once a Celtic nation but now is a county in England's southwestern corner. Breton is still spoken by about 250,000 people in Brittany, in western France.

Where is Hadrian's Wall?

What's left of Hadrian's wall—originally about 73 miles (117 km) long—is in northern England, south of the Scottish border. This massive stone wall was ordered built by the Roman emperor Hadrian almost 2,000 years ago to mark the northern boundary of the Roman empire.

What is the Chunnel?

The Chunnel, short for Channel Tunnel, is actually three tunnels—two train tunnels and a central service tunnel—that connect England and France. It was completed in 1994 and extends for 31 miles (28 km), most of which run under the English Channel. Trains that run 100 miles per hour (161 km/hr) take just 20 minutes to make the trip between the two countries.

The thousands of tons of chalky earth that were removed to create the Chunnel were used to build a 90-acre (36-hectare) park in England.

Countries in which two or more languages are widely spoken are called poly-glot states.

Why is Belgium called a divided country?

Two distinct groups of people live in Belgium. The northern part of the country, closer to the Netherlands, is called Flanders. The people who live there are Flemings, and they speak a language similar to Dutch called Flemish.

The southern part of Belgium, closer to France, is called Walloonia. The people who live there are called Walloons, and they speak French. Even the capital city of Brussels has French and Flemish zones. Only about 1 Belgian in 10 speaks both languages.

Which is the correct name of the country on the North Sea: Holland or the Netherlands?

Netherlands, or the Netherlands, is the proper name of the country on the North Sea that borders Belgium and Germany. "Holland" is sometimes used to mean the Netherlands, but technically it is the name of a region in the western part of the country.

About one-fourth of the Netherlands lies below sea level. For nearly 2,000 years, the Dutch people have had to build dikes, dams, and dunes to keep their land from being swallowed up by the sea.

How does France compare in size and economy with other countries in Europe and the world?

It's the third largest European country in land area, behind Russia and Ukraine. From a U.S. perspective, it's somewhat smaller than Texas. It is the world's fourth largest economy, after the United States, Japan, and Germany.

France is the top tourist destination in the world, followed by Spain, the United States, and Italy. It is also a leading manufacturing and agricultural country. Its automobile, steel, and chemical industries are among the largest in the world.

Which is taller: the Eiffel Tower in Paris, France, or the Washington Monument in Washington, D.C.?

The Eiffel Tower is almost twice as tall as the Washington Monument. It rises 985 feet (300 m) near the

Seine River, while the Washington Monument stands at 555 feet (169 m) near the Potomac River.

Where, and what, are the Pillars of Hercules?

The Pillars of Hercules is the ancient name for two huge rocks that stand on either side of the Strait of Gibraltar, which separates Spain from Africa. The waters of the Atlantic Ocean flow east through the strait into the Mediterranean Sea.

One of those rocks is Gibraltar, a territory of the United Kingdom; the other is Jebel Musa in Africa. The Rock of Gibraltar is a huge limestone promontory that lies on a peninsula off the coast of southern Spain. Gibraltar is only 2.5 square miles (6.5 sq km), but its prime location on the Strait of Gibraltar has long made it a valuable piece of land for military reasons.

The British took Gibraltar from Spain in a 1704 war. Spain would like to have Gibraltar back, but so far the United Kingdom has refused to return it.

Is Spain mainly a plain?

Spain is mainly a high plateau called the Meseta that is covered with plains and a few low mountains. Nearly three-fourths of the country, which occupies the Iberian Peninsula with Portugal, is almost always sunny and dry, except for some rain in the winter. Spain is separated from France by the Pyrenees Mountains to the northeast.

Was there really such a place as Atlantis?

A French geologist thinks that the legend of Atlantis, a mythical island city that sank under the ocean, may have a basis in fact. About 11,000 years ago, when the last ice age ended, a small island sat in what is now the Strait of Gibraltar, south of Spain. When the ice melted, the sea levels rose, and over a 300-year period the island became completely submerged. He believes it now lies as deep as 400 feet (122 m) under water. Stories about this event may have been told and retold over the centuries until the Atlantis legend took shape.

Portugal is home to one-third of the world's cork oak forests, and the country produces more than half the world's cork. Cork is harvested once every 10 years from cork oak trees by stripping the bark from the lower part of the tree.

What was the first city in the world to have 1 million people?

Rome, Italy, was the first city with 1 million people, back in the first century B.C. It took nearly 2,000 years for the next world city to reach that number—London, England, in 1810. Today, nearly 300 cities around the world have populations of more than a million people.

Is it true that Venice, Italy, is slowly sinking into the sea?

Yes, Venice is slowly sinking, or subsiding, into the marshy ground on which it was built beginning more than a thousand years ago. Some U.S. scientists believe that it has subsided about 9.3 inches (24 cm) in the past century. Frequent flooding caused by storms and high tides is causing building foundations to erode, making matters worse. Air pollution is also damaging Venetian buildings.

The city of Venice, Italy, is famed for its canals. All traffic in the city is carried on gondolas or boats; no cars or trucks are permitted.

Venice's famous Piazza San Marco, the lowest point in the city, floods as many as 100 times a year—much more frequently than in the past. Rising sea levels, a result of climate change, are contributing to the problem.

The city is planning to build a series of movable dams to protect Venice from flood waters. But the project is controversial, and many think the dams won't solve the problem.

Venice lies on about 120 small islands in a lagoon on the Adriatic Sea. Its beautiful old buildings sit on top of millions of wooden pilings. Cars and trucks are not allowed in the city; instead, people and goods move around by boat on canals.

Is the world's oldest republic in Europe?

Yes. The tiny country of San Marino is the oldest republic in the world: it was founded in the 300s. It lies entirely within the country of Italy, in the Apennine Mountains.

Which countries do the Alps Mountains cross?

Switzerland, Austria, Liechtenstein, Germany, Italy, and Slovenia are the major countries that lie within the 660-mile (1,060-m) crescent of the Alps mountain range, Europe's largest. The countries of Croatia, Bosnia and Herzegovina, Yugoslavia, and Albania also have portions of the Alps (called the Dinaric Alps) within their boundaries.

For thousands of years, travelers had a difficult time crossing the Alps. The Romans built the first roads through the passes 2,000 years ago so they could trade with their provinces in northern Europe. Today, six major tunnels cut through the mountains, making travel quick and easy throughout this scenic region.

Is Greece mostly made up of islands?

No, only about one-fifth of Greece's land area is made up of its 2,000 or so islands in the Aegean and Ionian Seas, which are part of the larger Mediterranean Sea. The largest of these islands is Crete. The country's mainland lies on the tip of the Balkan Peninsula and is surrounded

Huge glaciers formed the many dramatic large lakes in the Alps, including Lakes Lucerne, Como, Maggiore, Geneva, Constance, and Zurich. About 1,300 small glaciers remain scattered throughout the Alps today.

The word alps is also used to describe similar mountain ranges around the world—for example, the Australian Alps and New Zealand's Southern Alps.

on the east, south, and west by the sea. Much of inland Greece is mountainous.

Greece is called the birthplace of Western civilization. More than 2,500 years ago, the ancient Greeks introduced the idea of democratic government, and they laid the groundwork for future civilizations in the areas of art, science, and philosophy.

Is there really a place called Transylvania?

Yes, Transylvania is a province of Romania that sits atop a plateau in the central part of the country. The model for the legendary Count Dracula, Vlad Tepes (also known as Vlad the Impaler), a real Wallachian prince, carried out his atrocities in this region in the 1400s. Transylvania is bordered by the Transylvanian Alps and the Carpathian Mountains.

Which countries made up the old Soviet Union?

The Soviet Union, which dissolved in 1991 after the collapse of its Communist government, was officially the Union of Soviet Socialist Republics (USSR). It contained Russia and today's independent countries of Armenia, Azerbaijan, Belarus, Estonia, Georgia, Kazakhstan, Kyrgyzstan, Latvia, Lithuania, Moldova, Russia, Tajikistan, Turkmenistan, Ukraine, and Uzbekistan.

What is the Russian Federation?

This is Russia's offical name. The Russian Federation, which occupies about three-fourths of the land that once was the Soviet Union, is made up of 21 autonomous republics, 50 oblasts (or regions), 6 krays (or provinces), 2 federal cities (Moscow and St. Petersburg), 1 autonomous oblast, and 10 autonomous okrugs (or autonomous territories).

How many time zones does Russia have?

Russia spreads out over such a large area that it covers 11 time zones. The Continental United States, in comparison, has 4 time zones.

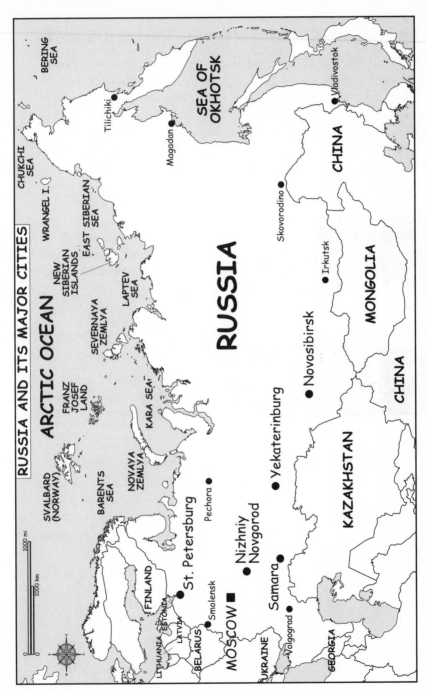

RUSSIA AND ITS MAJOR CITIES

Russia is one of the world's largest countries, stretching from Europe to Asia. Most of its people live in the western part, in the European portion.

The Fall of Communism in Eastern Europe

The year 1989 was the beginning of the end of Communist governments in several eastern European countries. People in Poland, Hungary, Albania, Bulgaria, Czechoslovakia, Yugoslavia, Romania, the German Democratic Republic, and elsewhere began demanding rights and freedoms that had been suppressed under Communism.

In 1989, the Berlin Wall, the symbolic structure separating Communist East Germany from West Germany, fell, and Germany reunified the following year.

By the early 1990s, Yugoslavia and Czechoslovakia broke apart along religious and ethnic lines and several new countries were formed. Yugoslavia today is now only the republics of Serbia and Montenegro. The former Yugoslav republics of Bosnia and Herzegovina, Macedonia, Slovenia, and Croatia are independent countries.

In 1993, Czechoslovakia split into the two countries that are now called the Czech Republic and the Slovak Republic.

Is there still a country named Prussia?

No, although there once was. After World War II, Poland, Germany, and Russia each took parts of Prussia and added them to their lands.

Which countries make up the Balkan states?

Albania, Bosnia and Herzegovina, Bulgaria, Croatia, Greece, Macedonia, Romania, Slovenia, and Yugoslavia, as well as a small part of Turkey, all lie on the Balkan Peninsula. Part of Greece is also on the Balkan Peninsula but Greece is not considered to be one of the Balkan states.

What countries make up the Baltic states?

Estonia, Latvia, and Lithuania all touch the Baltic Sea. These three countries declared their independence from the Soviet Union in 1990.

Is Russia in Asia or Europe? ◆ Is the Middle East in Asia? ◆ Which countries make up the Middle East? ◆ Is the Middle East mostly desert? ◆ How do people manage to grow crops in such an arid environment? ◆ Where is the region known as The Cradle of Civilization? ◆ Who are the Arab people? ◆ What religions are practiced in the Middle East? ◆ Why is the Middle East important to the rest of the world? ◆ Which world countries are the leading producers of oil? ◆ How much does the United States depend on oil from the Middle East? ◆ Which part of Turkey lies in Europe? ◆ Where is Mount Ararat? ◆ Who are the Kurds? ◆ Is the Red Sea really red? ◆ Do any marine animals live in

CHAPTER 5

ASIA

Is Russia in Asia or Europe?

Russia is so large that it straddles both continents. Most of Russia's huge land area lies in Asia, but most of its people live in the western portion of the country, which is in eastern Europe. (See more about Russia on page 80.)

Is the Middle East in Asia?

Yes, geographically the Middle East is a region in southwest Asia. Countries in northern Africa, in particular Egypt and Sudan, are often considered to be part of the Middle East as well.

Which countries make up the Middle East?

Geographers sometimes disagree on this point, but most place the following countries in the Middle East: Bahrain, Cyprus, Egypt, Iran, Iraq, Israel, Jordan, Kuwait, Lebanon, Oman, Qatar, Saudi Arabia, Sudan, Syria, Turkey, the United Arab Emirates, and Yemen.

Is the Middle East mostly desert?

Yes, about two-thirds of the land in the Middle East is desert. A desert is an area that receives less than 10 inches (25 cm) of precipitation a year.

The world's largest sand desert is the Sahara, in northern Africa. The largest *continuous* area of sand in the

Kazakhstan, one of five central Asian states that declared its independence from the Soviet Union in 1991, is almost four times the size of Texas and ranks as the ninth largest country in the world.

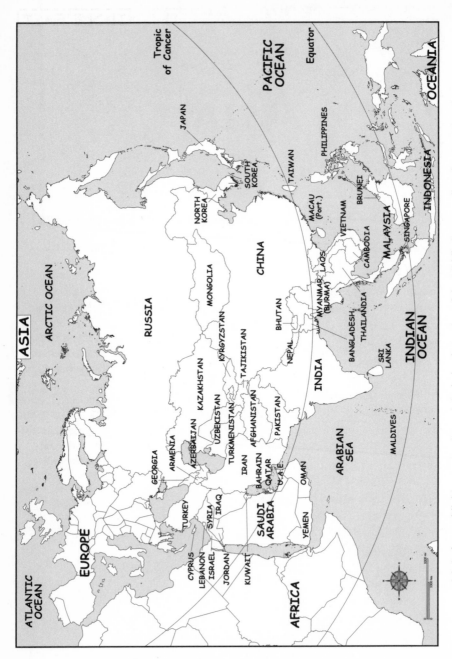

ASIA

ATLANTIC OCEAN

EUROPE

ARCTIC OCEAN

RUSSIA

Tropic of Cancer

JAPAN

NORTH KOREA

SOUTH KOREA

MONGOLIA

CHINA

TAIWAN

PACIFIC OCEAN

Equator

GEORGIA
ARMENIA
AZERBAIJAN
KAZAKHSTAN
UZBEKISTAN
KYRGYZSTAN
TAJIKISTAN
TURKMENISTAN
AFGHANISTAN
PAKISTAN

TURKEY
SYRIA
IRAQ
IRAN

CYPRUS
LEBANON
ISRAEL
JORDAN
KUWAIT

BAHRAIN
QATAR
U.A.E.

OMAN

YEMEN

SAUDI ARABIA

AFRICA

NEPAL
BHUTAN
BANGLADESH

INDIA

MYANMAR (BURMA)
LAOS
THAILAND
CAMBODIA
VIETNAM
MACAU (Port.)

PHILIPPINES

BRUNEI
MALAYSIA
SINGAPORE

INDONESIA

OCEANIA

SRI LANKA

MALDIVES

ARABIAN SEA

INDIAN OCEAN

1000 km
500 mi

Asia is the world's biggest continent. It includes the region of the Middle East as well as the countries of India, China, Indonesia, and Japan. Asia is one of the most culturally diverse places on Earth.

84

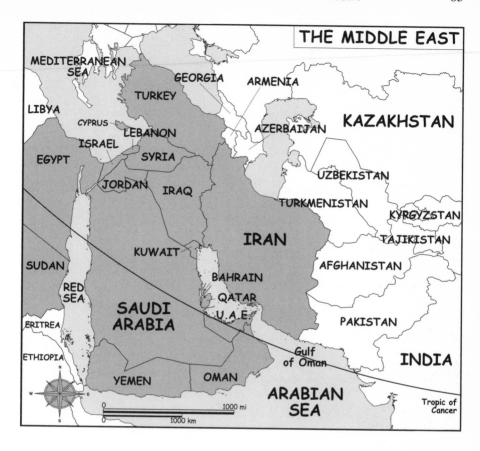

THE MIDDLE EAST

MEDITERRANEAN SEA
GEORGIA
ARMENIA
TURKEY
LIBYA
CYPRUS
LEBANON
ISRAEL
AZERBAIJAN
KAZAKHSTAN
EGYPT
SYRIA
JORDAN
IRAQ
UZBEKISTAN
TURKMENISTAN
KYRGYZSTAN
TAJIKISTAN
IRAN
SUDAN
KUWAIT
AFGHANISTAN
RED SEA
BAHRAIN
QATAR
ERITREA
SAUDI ARABIA
U.A.E.
PAKISTAN
ETHIOPIA
Gulf of Oman
INDIA
YEMEN
OMAN
ARABIAN SEA
Tropic of Cancer
1000 mi
1000 km

world—about the size of Texas—is a desert called the Rub'al-Khali, meaning "Empty Quarter," in Saudi Arabia. Temperature ranges in these deserts can go from 120°F (49°C) in the daytime to 40°F (4°C) at night.

The shaded area indicates the nations that most geographers agree constitute the Middle East.

How do people manage to grow crops in such an arid environment?

Irrigation has long been necessary for farming in the Middle East. Water from the region's two major river systems—the Nile and the Tigris-Euphrates—has made agriculture possible.

One unusual source of water for irrigation is the qanat system. For at least 2,000 years, people in the Middle East have dug underground tunnels that funnel water to their villages from wells in uphill areas. The qanat system has a big advantage over open canals in hot, dry areas: since the water is not exposed to the open air, less evaporation takes place.

Farmers in Iran and Oman still rely on qanats for some of their irrigation needs.

Where is the region known as the cradle of civilization?

In ancient times, the fertile valley between the Tigris and Euphrates Rivers in the area of today's Iraq was called Mesopotamia. It is often called the cradle of civilization because the development of agriculture there meant that people could live in one place year round. This stability eventually led to the creation of cities and governments.

The practice of agriculture—the planting of crops and the raising of livestock for food—was first developed about 10,000 years ago in the Middle East. Before that time, people had to keep moving to find food.

Because of the strict adherence to Islamic law in Saudi Arabia, women are not allowed to vote, nor are they allowed to drive a car or be seen in public with a man other than a close male relative. Numerous other restrictions are placed on Saudi women in school and at work. Women in many other Middle Eastern countries face similar restrictions, although some countries are more liberal than others.

Who are the Arab people?

Geographers define Arabs as people who speak the Arabic language and who usually, though not always, practice the Islamic religion. About 90 percent of the people who live in Middle Eastern countries and northern Africa are Arabic. Non-Arabs include Iranians, who speak Farsi (the ancient Persian language); Turks, who speak Turkish; and Kurds, who speak Kurdish.

Arabs make up most of the populations of Algeria, Egypt, Iraq, Jordan, Lebanon, Libya, Morocco, Saudi Arabia, Sudan, Syria, Tunisia, and Yemen.

What religions are practiced in the Middle East?

Most people—almost 9 out of 10—in the Middle East are Muslims, or followers of the Islamic religion. Most of these are Muslim Arabs. The Middle East is the birthplace of three major world religions: Islam, Christianity, and Judaism. But in the Middle East fewer than 1 out of 10 people are Christian, and about 1 in 100 people are Jewish.

Why is the Middle East so important to the rest of the world?

Because it contains most of the world's known oil reserves and is the world's top oil-producing region. Most of the oil produced in the Middle East is sold to countries in Asia and Europe.

Which world countries are the leading producers of oil?

In order, they are Saudi Arabia, the United States, Russia, Iraq, Iran, and Venezuela.

How much does the United States depend on oil from the Middle East?

The United States imports about half the oil it needs. Of that amount, about one-fifth comes from the Middle Eastern countries of Bahrain, Iran, Kuwait, Qatar, Saudi Arabia, and the United Arab Emirates.

Which part of Turkey lies in Europe?

A small part of Turkey lies in a region of southern Europe called Thrace, which also includes parts of Greece and Bulgaria. Most of Turkey is in the Middle East, on a mountainous peninsula called Anatolia.

Where is Mount Ararat?

In Turkey, where it is called Agri Dagi. At 17,011 feet (5,185 m), it is the highest mountain in the Middle East.

Istanbul's Many Names

Istanbul, Turkey's largest city, sits at a strategic location on the Bosporus Strait, where it has long controlled access to the Mediterranean and Black Seas. It was called Byzantium in its early years. In A.D. 196, the Romans captured the city and renamed it Augusta Antonina. About 150 years later, it was called New Rome by Constantine the Great, and soon after that it became Constantinopolis and later Constantinople. Turkey officially changed the city's name to Istanbul in 1930.

Mount Ararat is believed to be the landing place of Noah's ark, according to the biblical story.

Who are the Kurds?

The Kurds are a nation of about 25 million people without a country. Kurdistan is a region, not a country, that stretches along parts of today's Turkey, Syria, Iran, and Iraq. In Turkey, the Kurds make up about 20 percent of the population—about 12 million people. Unlike most people in the Middle East, the Kurds are not Arabic, but most of them practice the Islamic religion.

Damascus, Syria, is the oldest inhabited city on Earth. It has been a settlement since at least 6000 B.C.

The Kurds have been fighting for independence since the end of World War I, when their dream to become an independent state did not materialize. They have suffered from terrorism, discrimination, and human rights abuses for many years. The Kurds have not had their own country since the seventh century.

Is the Red Sea really red?

No one is sure how the Red Sea got its name, but some people think it is because the water looks red during the summer when a reddish-brown algae floats on the surface.

The Red Sea lies between northeastern Africa and the Arabian peninsula. The Suez Canal, at the northern end of the Red Sea, lets ships travel back and forth to the Mediterranean Sea. At the southern end of the Red Sea, ships have access to the Indian Ocean. At about 1,400 miles long (2,200 km), the Red Sea is one of the busiest waterways in the world.

Do any marine animals live in the Red Sea?

Yes. The Red Sea is home to one of the world's most diverse and colorful coral reef systems. Many forms of marine life thrive there, including Napoleon wrasse, orange coral groupers, gorgonian fans, moray eels, hammerhead sharks, dramatic-looking lionfish, and giant manta rays.

Why is the Israeli city of Jerusalem always in the news?

Jerusalem has long been considered a holy city by three religions: Judaism, Christianity, and Islam. People of each religion have been struggling for control of the city for hundreds of years.

Jerusalem was founded by the Jewish king David about 3,100 years ago. About 2,000 years ago, Jesus Christ was born nearby and spent much of his life there. Muslims, people who practice Islam, consider the city to be holy because they believe that their founder, Mohammed, rose to heaven from Jerusalem.

Most of the people who live in Jerusalem today— about three-fourths of the population—are Jewish. The rest are Muslims and a few Christians.

The Palestinian people, who are Muslims, believe that Jerusalem is their traditional capital. They are hoping to establish their own country, even though there has never been an independent state of Palestine.

How did the Dead Sea get its name?

The Dead Sea is really a lake, not a sea, because it is surrounded by land. It is six times as salty as ocean water, and only a few forms of plant and animal life—mainly brine shrimp—can survive in the lake. It is salty because water never leaves the lake except by evaporation, a process that leaves behind deposits of salt and other minerals.

The Dead Sea, which forms part of the border between Israel and Jordan, is 50 miles (80 km) long and 11 miles (18 km) wide at its widest point. Its elevation is about 1,300 feet (400 m) below sea level, making it the lowest point on the planet.

Kuwait: From Rags to Riches

Kuwait, a desert country abut the size of New Jersey at the northern end of the Persian Gulf, has gone from being one of the world's poorest countries to one of the richest, thanks to its immense reserves of oil.

Kuwait has almost one-tenth of the known petroleum reserves in the world. About two-thirds of the people who live in Kuwait are workers from other countries—mostly from India, Egypt, and Bangladesh.

Where is Mecca?

Mecca is located in Saudi Arabia. It is the holiest city of the Islamic religion because it is where Islam's founder, Mohammed, was born in A.D. 571.

Muslims, the people who practice Islam, must make a pilgrimage to Mecca at least once in their lives. Muslims also must face toward Mecca while saying their daily prayers.

If you are not a Muslim, you are not allowed to visit Mecca. Today, Mecca is a city of half a million people.

What spot on the earth's land is farthest from an ocean?

A spot in northwestern China, near the borders of Russia and Mongolia, is more than 1,600 miles (2,575 km) from any ocean. Its latitude is 46°17' north, and its longitude is 86°40' east.

Even though most of the bananas we eat come from Central and South America, the banana is actually native to Asia. Banana plants were brought to the Americas by European colonists.

Do people in South Asian countries drive on the left side of the road or the right?

People in Bangladesh, Bhutan, Brunei, India, Indonesia, Japan, Malaysia, the Maldives, Nepal, Pakistan, Singapore, Sri Lanka, and Thailand drive on the left, as they do in the United Kingdom. Everyone else drives on the right, as in the United States. In the world overall, many more people drive on the right than on the left.

Where is the Khyber Pass?

The Khyber Pass cuts through the mountains on the border of Pakistan and Afghanistan. It's been used for hundreds of years by traders as well as by invaders. The pass is about 33 miles (53 km) long.

The suffix "-stan" at the end of several Asian country names means "nation" or "land." For example, Afghanistan means "Land of the Afghans."

How did Pakistan get its name?

Pakistan is a relatively new country, and it got its name in an unusual way. Its letters come from the first letters of the country's homelands: Punjab, Afghania, Kashmir, Iran, Sindh, Tukharistan, Afghanistan, and Balochistan (not for its first letter but for the last).

The countries of East and West Pakistan were carved out of India in 1947 to settle religious differences between

A Snapshot of India

With just over 1 billion people, India is the world's largest democracy. It has almost tripled in population since its independence from the United Kingdom in 1947.

India is the seventh largest country in the world in land area—it's about one-third the size of the United States—but it is the second largest country in number of people. One out of every six people in the world today lives in India. Only China has more people, but India is growing so fast that it may surpass China in population by 2035.

India is an incredibly varied country. Its people represent hundreds of nationalities and ethnic groups, and many different languages are spoken there. India is still one of the poorest countries in Asia, and millions of people live a meager existence in slums in its huge cities. Two of the world's largest cities are in India: Bombay (Mumbai), with 18 million people, and Calcutta (Kolkata), with 13 million.

India's landscapes range from the Himalayas in the north to desert areas in the west. Elsewhere there are hills, plains, rain forests, and tropical areas.

the Hindu majority and the Muslim minority. East and West Pakistan became the homeland for Muslim Indians. Several years later, East Pakistan declared its independence and became the nation of Bangladesh. West Pakistan then became known simply as Pakistan.

What language do people speak in India?

India has 18 official languages, but its people speak nearly 100 other languages and hundreds more dialects. Most Indians—about 40 percent—speak Hindi. The other Indian languages are largely regional. For example, most people in the Punjab state speak Punjabi. English is officially the "associate national language" and is widely used in business and government.

Why was the Taj Mahal built?

The Taj Mahal was built in honor of an Indian empress named Mumtaz Mahal. When she died at an early age, her husband was so grief-stricken that he decided to build a monument to her memory. In 1648, after 22 years

If Uttar Pradesh, one of India's 25 states, were an independent country, it would be the world's sixth largest in population. It has 150 million people.

Built in 1648 by the grieving widower of Indian empress Mumtaz Mahal, the white marble Taj Mahal is one of the most recognizable buildings in the world.

of work, the white marble structure on the banks of the Yamuna River in India was completed.

What's the difference between Asian elephants and African elephants?

African elephants are larger; in fact, they're the largest land animals on Earth. African elephants can weigh up to 8 tons (7,500 kg) and stand about 10 to 13 feet tall at the shoulder. Asian (or Indian) elephants are slightly shorter and weigh about 6 tons (5,500 kg). Probably the easiest way to tell the difference between Asian and African elephants is to compare the size of their ears: the Asian elephant's ears are much smaller.

People in Asia use elephants for logging and other work purposes. In Africa, elephants continued to be killed by humans for their ivory tusks. As humans in both Africa and Asia expand their settlements, both types of elephants are losing places to live. The Asian elephant is an endangered species, and the African elephant is a threatened species. International organizations use the term "endangered" to refer to animals and plants currently in danger of becoming extinct; "threatened" species are those that are likely to become endangered in the foreseeable future if preventive measures are not taken.

What is meant by the "Green Revolution" in India?

The Green Revolution took place between 1967 and 1978 in India and other parts of the developing world. It refers to improvements in agricultural practices that dramatically increased food production, especially wheat and rice in India.

By the 1960s, India was growing so fast that it could not produce enough food to keep up with the number of people. The government stepped in and began to develop more farmland and introduced modern irrigation systems, making it possible for farmers to plant two crops a year instead of one.

Indian farmers also planted genetically improved seeds that greatly increased crop yields. Within a decade, India had become one of the world's largest producers of farm products. In some years, farmers produced more food grains than the Indian people needed, so they sold the excess to other countries.

India has lost half its forests since 1950.

Bollywood is a nickname for the city of Mumbai (formerly Bombay). The name is a play on "Hollywood" and "Bombay." Bollywood is one of the world's largest film production centers.

How new is New Delhi?

New Delhi dates to 1931. It was built by the British, who ruled India at the time, because they wanted a new capital city. They built it next to the old capital of Delhi and so named it New Delhi.

How many people in India don't know how to read or write?

About one-third of India's men and two-thirds of its women are illiterate. India has a 12-year school system, but high school is optional. Only 38 percent of Indian girls and 59 percent of boys attend high school.

Is Tibet officially a country?

No. Tibet's official name is the Autonomous Region of the People's Republic of China. China has claimed Tibet as a territory since 1906, when the British turned Tibet over to China as part of a peace treaty. The Tibetans declared their independence from the Chinese just five years later. In 1950, China invaded Tibet, and hundreds of thousands of Tibetans fled to other countries or were killed.

Reports of human rights abuses continue today in Tibet, which is still under Chinese rule. Tibet's traditional religious and governmental ruler, the Dalai Lama, has been living in exile in India since 1959.

Nepal is one of the poorest nations on Earth. More than half its people live in extreme poverty.

Is Mount Everest in Tibet or Nepal?

It lies in both countries. The earth's tallest mountain, part of the Himalayas, lies on the border of Tibet and Nepal. Mount Everest is 29,035 feet (8,850 m)—about 5.5 miles—above sea level. The Nepalese name for Mount Everest is Sagarmatha, while the Tibetans call it Chomolungma.

The Himalaya mountains are still being formed because the Indian-Australian tectonic plate (on which India sits) continues to slowly push under the Eurasian plate. For this reason, Mount Everest and other Himalayan peaks will probably rise in height slightly for years to come.

Why does Bangladesh suffer so much from cyclones and floods?

Bangladesh's geographic location invites destruction from storms and floods. Much of the country is a flat alluvial plain, and most of its land is less than 50 feet (15 m) above sea level. As a result, the country is vulnerable to the full force of cyclones (hurricanes) and tsunami (huge waves caused by earthquakes) that strike it from the Bay of Bengal. The country also receives large amounts of rain during its monsoon season, and flooding is a constant threat.

Bangladesh is one of the most densely populated and poorest countries in the world. About 128 million people live in an area about the size of Wisconsin (a U.S. state that has about 5 million people). When storms and floods come, most people have nowhere to go for safety. One of the worst disasters took place in 1970, when a cyclone killed 300,000 people.

One reason that flooding in Bangladesh may be getting worse is that people in Nepal, several hundred miles north, have been cutting down trees in large forest areas

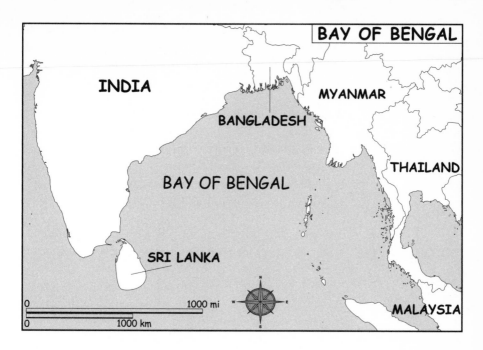

in the Himalayan foothills. Without vegetation to catch the water, the rains that fall during monsoon season run downstream into Bangladesh's rivers, increasing flooding there.

The Bay of Bengal lies to the east of India. Areas around it are subject to strong winds and rainstorms known as monsoons.

What is a monsoon?

A monsoon is a shift in wind direction. In Asia, the monsoon season runs from May to September, when Southern Hemisphere winds shift direction and blow north and west across the Equator into Asia, bringing moisture from the oceans they pass over on the way.

Monsoon winds bring much-needed rain, which farmers depend on for their crops. But flooding often results when the ground has been hard and dry for many months and cannot absorb the sudden heavy rainfall.

How large is Mongolia?

Mongolia, a country in Asia bordered by China and Russia, has about 1.5 times the land area of California. But only 2.5 million people live there—about the same number who live in the St. Louis, Missouri, metropolitan area. Only 1 percent of the land in Mongolia is suitable for farming.

How many people live in China?

About 1.26 billion people lived in China in 2001, more than four times the number of people who lived in the United States. The total land area of both countries is about the same. China has the most people of any country on Earth, although India is not far behind.

Is it true that the Great Wall of China is the only artificial structure that can be seen from low Earth orbit?

No, it's not the only one. Many human-made objects can be seen with the naked eye from the space shuttle. For example, astronauts can look out their windows and see highways, railroads, and even bridges.

But once space vehicles climb a few thousand miles above Earth, astronauts cannot see any human-made objects on the planet.

Writing in Chinese

For at least 3,500 years, the Chinese have used pictures rather than letters to write things down. This type of writing is called pictography. A symbol represents a word in this system, which has about 50,000 different characters. Only about 4,000 are used for everyday writing, though.

The interesting thing about the Chinese language is that even though it has hundreds of regional dialects and many different ways of pronouncing the same word, all Chinese people can read and understand written Chinese.

In the late 1950s, the Chinese introduced a phonetic way of writing, using the Roman alphabet, called the Pinyin system. With this system, the Chinese people can communicate more easily with other world languages. Under this system, for example, the city we used to call Peking is now called Beijing, which is closer to the way the Chinese pronounce the name.

EAST ASIA

JAPAN

NORTH
KOREA

P'yongyang•
•Seoul

Beijing•

SOUTH
KOREA

CHINA

Chengdu •
• Chongqing

Taipei•

BHUTAN

TAIWAN

Guengzhou•
•Hong Kong

Hanoi•
MYANMAR   •Haiphong
(BURMA) LAOS

PHILIPPINES

Vientiane•

VIETNAM

THAILAND

Bangkok•
CAMBODIA

Phnom Penh•

MALAYSIA

INDONESIA

1000 mi

1000 km

How old and how big is the Great Wall of China?

The first part of the Great Wall was built about 2,000 years ago as a way to keep people from Mongolia from entering China. Until the 1600s, many more sections were built and rebuilt, until the wall and its branches eventually spread out over 4,000 miles, from Korea in the east to the Gobi Desert in the west.

The main portion is about 1,500 miles (2,415 km) long. It was built entirely by hand of brick, dirt, and stone. The first section was constructed at the rate of 1 mile (1.6

East Asia is one of the most densely populated areas on Earth. China alone has more than four times the population of the United States.

To support such a huge population, the Chinese must use their farmland efficiently. They plant more than 90 percent of it with crops meant for people, not livestock. (More than 50 percent of all U.S. farmland is used to grow food for livestock.) As a result, the Chinese eat very little meat compared with people in the United States.

km) per day, an astonishing rate of accomplishment. It is the world's longest artificial structure.

How many times zones are there in China?

One. China does not use time zones, even though the country does stretch across five of them. Clocks all over China are set to the same time: 8 hours ahead of Greenwich Mean Time.

Does Hong Kong belong to the United Kingdom or China?

Since 1997, Hong Kong has been a territory of China. Prior to that date, the island of Hong Kong had been a colony of the United Kingdom for 56 years. Since China ceded the island to Britain in 1942, part of what is now Hong Kong is on the Chinese mainland. China gave Britain a 99-year lease on this area in 1898. That lease expired in 1997.

Which is China's longest river: the Yangtze or the Yellow?

The Yangtze River runs for about 3,955 miles (6,363 km), and is longer than the Yellow River, which is about 2,896 miles (4,660 km) long. The Yangtze is the world's third longest river, after the Nile and the Amazon. The Yellow River is the world's seventh longest.

What is the Three Gorges Dam?

It is China's largest construction project since the Great Wall. The Three Gorges Dam, when it is completed in 2003, will be 1.5 miles wide and 600 feet (183 m) high, stretching across the Yangtze River. It will take another six years to completely fill the 350-mile-long (563-km) lake created by the dam.

Supporters of the Three Gorges Dam say it will have many important benefits. It will create huge amounts of low-cost electricity for the surrounding region, help control devastating floods on the lower part of the Yangtze River, and allow oceangoing ships to come into China's interior, boosting economic development there. They say that the dam will benefit the environment because it will generate

How Burning Coal in China Kills Trees in Japan

Most of China's energy is produced by burning coal, which spews sulfur and nitrogen compounds into the air, where they combine with moisture and become acidic. These particles eventually fall back to Earth, and some are often carried westward for hundreds of miles by wind and rainstorms. Japan, located just a few hundred miles west of China, has suffered because of acid rain that had its origins in China.

Acid rain can damage plant life—in Japan's case, pine and fir trees in particular—and can also cause health problems in humans. China and Japan are trying to work together to solve this problem. Other countries affected by Chinese air pollution are North Korea, South Korea, and Vietnam.

clean hydroelectric power, making it possible to shut down many coal-burning power plants, which pollute the air.

But many people are against the dam, for various reasons. The Chinese government must find new homes for the 1 million people whose towns and villages will be underwater when the dam is completed. More than 100 ancient archaeological sites will be lost forever.

Many others fear that the dam is not being built properly and will collapse and cause a great catastrophe. Others say the dam will lead to environmental damage in the region, in particular increased water pollution resulting from the dam's construction and the growing number of industrial plants in the area.

Why isn't Taiwan a member of the United Nations?

When the People's Republic of China—what we think of as the country of China—was admitted to the United Nations in 1971, it demanded that Taiwan be removed as a member. Taiwan, which calls itself the Republic of China (it's also known as Nationalist China), has considered itself to be a separate nation since 1949.

China disagrees—it considers Taiwan to be one of its provinces and would like to regain control of the island, which it lost to Japan in a war in 1895.

Taiwan has about 22 million people and lies about

100 miles off the coast of mainland China. It is a major world exporter of high-tech products.

The Korean language is unlike any other language in the world. Some experts believe it belongs to the same language family as Japanese, although about half its words are Chinese in origin.

Why are there two Koreas?

Japan controlled Korea from 1910 until 1945. At the end of World War II, Korea was divided into two countries, one of which had a Communist government: North Korea, formally called the Democratic People's Republic of Korea. South Korea is a non-Communist country that elects its leaders. The two countries have about the same land area, but South Korea has almost twice as many people as North Korea.

The two Koreas are officially still at war, since a peace treaty was never signed when the conflict between them ended in 1953. In recent years, some progress has been made in opening up communication and travel between the two countries.

How many islands make up the country of Japan?

Japan consists of 3,000 islands—called an archipelago—that extend over 1,500 miles (2,415 km) in the central and south Pacific. In total land area, Japan is about the size of the state of Montana. Most of the country's 126 million people live on one of its four main islands. The majority live on Honshu, the largest island. The other three large islands are Shikoku, Kyushu, and Hokkaido.

About 80 percent of Japan's land area is mountainous, so most people live in the valleys and coastal areas. As a result, Japan's population density is one of the highest in the world—869 people per square mile.

Is Mount Fuji an active volcano?

Yes. Mount Fuji is a volcanic mountain that last erupted in 1708. Its peak stands at 12,388 feet (3,776 m) above sea level. It is the most visited mountain in the world. More than 100,000 people climb it each year in July and August—its two-month climbing season.

What was the worst natural disaster to hit Japan?

In 1923, an earthquake struck near Tokyo and Yokohama, killing more than 130,000 people and destroying most of both cities.

More recently, in 1995, the city of Kōbe, Japan, was devastated by a powerful 7.2-magnitude earthquake that killed more than 6,400 people.

Volcanoes have also caused destruction in Japan. In 1792, the dome of the Unzen volcano, near Kyushu, collapsed, causing a volcanic landslide. When the landslide fell into the sea, it in turn caused a huge tsunami, which destroyed several coastal villages and killed 15,000 people.

A tsunami is a very large wave caused by the actions of earthquakes, landslides, or rarely, as in the Unzen volcano, by island volcanoes. The Unzen volcano became active again in the 1990s.

Japan has the world's second largest economy, after that of the United States.

What was the highest tsunami ever recorded?

The highest tsunami on record took place in Lituya Bay, Alaska, in 1958. This tsunami was not caused by an earthquake but by a massive landslide that fell into the bay. The wave that resulted was 1,700 feet (518 m) high.

Is Tokyo the largest city on Earth?

Yes, Tokyo had 33.1 million people in 2000, much larger than the next-largest cities of New York City and Seoul-Inchon, Korea. (See page 25 for a list of the world's largest cities.)

Fewer babies are born to women in Japan than in almost any other country. But girls born there today can expect to live to be 84 years old—the highest life expectancy in the world.

Is there still a country in southeast Asia called Siam?

Since 1939, Siam has been called Thailand, which means "Land of the Free." Siam had been the country's

Yangon's Incredible Jeweled Temple

The Shwedagon Pagoda, a Buddhist temple that sits on a hill in the Myanmar capital of Yangon, has a tall spire that is covered with thousands of plates of gold and topped with more than 5,400 diamonds and 2,300 rubies, sapphires, and other precious stones. The temple dates back more than 2,000 years.

Before 1989, when a military regime took over the government, Myanmar was known as Burma, and Yangon was called Rangoon. Today, few tourists visit Shwedagon Pagoda and other ancient sites because of Myanmar's reputation as a dangerous place for foreigners.

Of all the countries in southeast Asia, Thailand is the only one that was never colonized by a European country.

Angkor Wat in Cambodia, built more than 900 years ago, is the largest complex of religious buildings in the world. All the buildings make up one huge Hindu temple.

name for 700 years. In land area, Thailand is about the size of Texas.

Thailand's capital, Bangkok, is sometimes called the "Venice of the East" because of its canals; the city sits on an island in the Chao Phraya River. This city of close to 9 million people is both modern and ancient, with more than 300 Buddhist temples and monasteries sitting alongside modern office buildings. It's also one of the world's most congested and polluted cities.

Where is the temple of Angkor Wat?

Angkor Wat, a Hindu temple that is the world's largest grouping of religious buildings, is in Cambodia. Made of thousands of tons of carved stone, the temple's 600 buildings were built in the 1100s.

Malaysia: A Country Split in Two

Malaysia, a country in southeast Asia, is unusual geographically because it consists of two separate land areas that are 400 miles (644 km) apart, across the South China Sea. One part sits on the Malay Peninsula, the location of Kuala Lumpur, the nation's capital. The other part of the country occupies the northern and northwestern coasts of the island of Borneo.

Is Vietnam still divided into North and South, like Korea?

No, it has been unified since 1976. In that year the Communists of North Vietnam defeated South Vietnam after nearly 20 years of war and it became one country, called the Socialist Republic of Vietnam. The United States was involved in that war, in which 58,000 Americans died.

Vietnam is long and narrow in shape: it is more than 1,000 miles (1,610 km) long but only about 380 miles (612 km) wide at its widest point.

Is Singapore a city or a country?

It's both. Singapore, which is smaller in area and population than New York City, was a British colony until 1959. Most of its citizens are Chinese. It occupies Singapore Island and 57 outlying islets off the Malay Peninsula.

Where is Indonesia?

Indonesia is a country on the Java Sea, along the Equator in Southeast Asia. It is unusual because it is made up entirely of islands—more than 13,000 of them, many of them volcanic and stretching over an area of 3,200 miles (5,152 km). People live on about 6,000 of those islands. Indonesia's islands form the largest archipelago in the world.

Sumatra and Java are two of the largest islands. Java has 112 mountains, 17 of which are active volcanoes. It is also one of the most densely populated islands in the

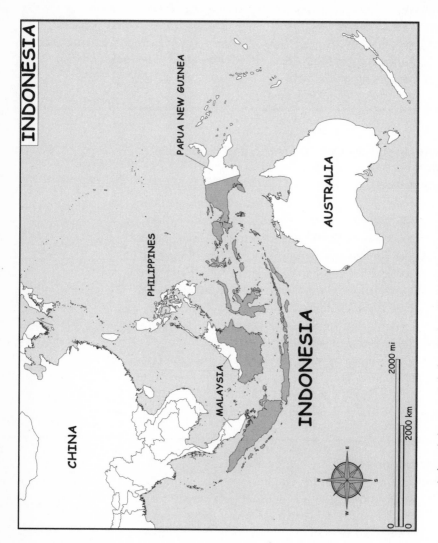

INDONESIA

CHINA

PHILIPPINES

PAPUA NEW GUINEA

MALAYSIA

INDONESIA

AUSTRALIA

2000 mi

2000 km

Indonesia is composed of more than 13,200 islands, the largest archipelago in the world. Numerous cultures flourish there, and more than 250 languages are spoken.

world. The fertile volcanic soils in the eastern part of Java let farmers grow up to three crops a year, which makes it possible for the country to feed all its people.

Indonesia is the fourth largest country in the world in population, after China, India, and the United States. It has 212 million people, most of whom are Muslims. For almost 300 years, Indonesia was governed by a European country, the Netherlands.

How many languages are spoken in Indonesia?

People in Indonesia speak more than 250 languages and belong to 300 different ethnic groups. In the 1920s, they devised a common language so they could communicate with one another. It is called Bahasa Indonesia, which is based on the Malay language.

Does the Philippines belong to the United States?

No, it became an independent country in 1946. The Philippines had been a U.S. territory since 1898, when the Spanish gave the islands to the United States at the end of the Spanish-American War. Spain had ruled the islands for the previous 300 years.

The Philippines consists of more than 7,000 islands, but its people live on only about 1,000 of them. They speak many languages, in particular a language called Tagalog. English is an official language.

How many countries are on the African continent? ◆ How
many people live in **CHAPTER 6** African country is the
largest in land area? ◆ Which African country is the smallest in land area? ◆ Which African country has the largest
population? ◆ Where are the Atlas Mountains? ◆ Which
country's flag is just a single block of color? ◆ Is it true that
children in some **AFRICA** are sent to fight in
wars? ◆ How large is the Sahara Desert? ◆ Is the Nile the
world's longest river? ◆ What is the difference between
the White Nile and the Blue Nile? ◆ Why is Egypt often
called a Middle Eastern country when it is actually on the
African continent? ◆ How large is the Aswan High Dam, or

How many countries are on the African continent?

Africa has 54 independent countries—48 in sub-
Saharan Africa and six in North Africa—as well as several
territories and other political units. These include eight
territories under French rule, one British island territory
(St. Helena), one Norwegian territory (Bouvet Island), one
Australian territory (Heard Island and McDonald Islands),
and one Spanish territory (the Canary Islands).

How many people live in Africa?

About 800 million people live in Africa—nearly three
times the number of people in the United States. It is the
world's second largest continent, both in land area and in
number of people, after Asia.

Africa's population is growing rapidly because
women in Africa are having nearly six children each, on
average. Women in the United States are having just two
children each, on average.

Which African country is the largest in land area?

Sudan covers 963,600 square miles (2,495,712 sq km),
an area larger than Alaska and Texas combined.

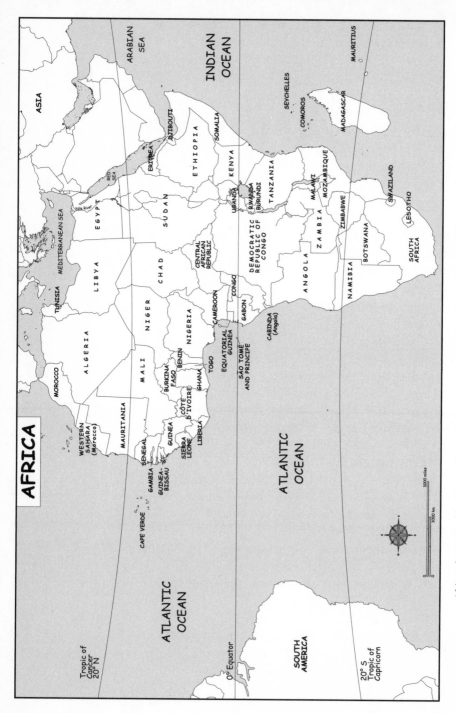

Africa, the second largest continent, is home to 54 countries. The Sudan is the largest in area, while Nigeria has the largest population—and one of the world's fastest growing, too.

Which African country is the smallest in land area?

Seychelles, a small group of islands in the Indian Ocean, has a land area of just 176 square miles (456 sq km).

Which African country has the largest population?

Nigeria has the largest population by far, with about 123 million people. It is one of the world's fastest growing countries—experts predict that by 2050 Nigeria will more than double in size, to about 300 million people. That would be about 20 million more people than live in the United States today.

Where are the Atlas Mountains?

The Atlas mountain range is Africa's longest, extending from Morocco to Tunisia in northern Africa. The chain is part of the mountain system that includes the Alps in Europe.

Which country's flag is just a single block of color?

Libya's flag is a solid green rectangle, with no design of any kind. Green is the country's national color, and it also indicates devotion to the Islamic religion.

Is it true that children in some African countries are sent to fight in wars?

Unfortunately, yes. Children as young as seven or eight years old serve in the military in several African countries (and elsewhere in the world), including Sierra Leone, Uganda, Liberia, Mozambique, Rwanda, Sudan, and the Democratic Republic of the Congo.

The United Nations is working to pass the U.N. Convention on the Rights of the Child, which would set 15 years as the minimum age for service in the armed forces.

How large is the Sahara Desert?

The Sahara Desert in northern Africa is the largest dry desert in the world; it covers one-third of the African continent. At about 3.5 million square miles (9 million sq km), it is almost as large as the contiguous 48 United States.

The Sahara grows larger every year, as the surrounding land dries up and turns into desert.

Another large desert in Africa is the Namib, which stretches along the southwest coast. It receives less than 6 inches of rain a year.

Is the Nile the world's longest river?

Yes. The Nile River flows northward for about 4,160 miles (6,693 km) through Sudan, Uganda, and Egypt into the Mediterranean Sea. Most of the Nile's water comes from Lake Victoria, which lies in the countries of Kenya, Tanzania, and Uganda.

What is the difference between the White Nile and the Blue Nile?

The White Nile runs between the Sudd, a huge swamp, and Khartoum, both in the country of Sudan. The Blue Nile runs through Ethiopia and joins with the White Nile south of Khartoum. From that point on, this great river is known simply as the Nile.

Why is Egypt often called a Middle Eastern country when it is actually on the African continent?

Because, like the rest of northern Africa, Egypt is populated mostly by people of Arabic descent. In fact, its official name is the Arab Republic of Egypt. Part of Egypt—the Sinai Peninsula—is really considered part of Asia, not Africa. This eastern part of the country borders on Israel, Jordan, and Saudi Arabia.

Egypt is the second largest country in population in Africa, after Nigeria. Its land area is about the same as Texas, Arkansas, and Oklahoma combined. Because so much of Egypt is desert, almost everyone lives either near the Nile River or along the Suez Canal. Cairo, Egypt's capital, is the largest city in Africa, with 10.6 million people.

How large is the Aswan High Dam, on the Nile River?

The Aswan High Dam in southern Egypt is 364 feet (111 m) tall and 12,565 feet (3,830 m) long. It was completed in 1970, after 10 years of construction. It is built of

The Suez Canal

The Suez Canal in Egypt connects the Mediterranean Sea and the Red Sea. It is the longest canal that does not require locks because the water levels of the Mediterranean and the Gulf of Suez are practically the same. (Locks are sections of a canal that are closed off by gates, allowing water levels to be adjusted so that ships can be raised or lowered to the proper level.) Before the canal was completed in 1869, ships had to sail around Africa in order to get to Asia and the Pacific Ocean. The 100-mile-long (161 km) canal cuts through the continents of Asia and Africa and carries 14 percent of the total world trade and 26 percent of oil exports.

The Suez Canal was built by a French and British company, and the British controlled the canal for many years. In 1956, the Egyptian president Gamal Nasser declared that the canal belonged to Egypt. He did this because the British, French, and American governments refused to give Egypt loans to build the Aswan High Dam. As a result, Great Britain, France, and Israel invaded Egypt. The United Nations stepped in, ordering those countries to leave and letting Egypt keep control of the canal.

silt, sand, clay, and rock—about 16 times as much material as contained in the Great Pyramid at Giza.

The dam was built for several reasons: to control flooding on the Nile, to increase Egypt's electricity generation, and to provide water for crop irrigation. The dam made it possible to transform about 100,000 acres (40,470 hectares) of desert into farmland.

Why are there so many wars between and within countries in Africa?

Africa is home to more than 800 ethnic groups, each of which has its own language, beliefs, and traditions. All of these groups lived in Africa long before Europeans founded colonies there in the 1800s.

The Europeans drew boundary lines for their territories without considering traditional regions, and as a result many ethnic groups were split up. Those arbitrary borders have made it hard for today's African countries—most of

SUEZ CANAL

MEDITERRANEAN
SEA

West Bank

ISRAEL

Gaza Strip

DEAD SEA

Port Said

SUEZ
CANAL

JORDAN

Cairo

Sinai

SAUDI
ARABIA

Nile River

E G Y P T

RED
SEA

LAKE
NASSER

LIBYA

350 miles

350 km

S U D A N

The Suez Canal links the Mediterranean and the Red Seas. It enables ships to pass from Europe to Asia and the Pacific without rounding the southern tip of Africa.

which became independent between 1950 and 1980—to form unified nations.

What languages are spoken in Africa?

In northern Africa, Arabic and Berber are the most widely spoken languages. In southern Africa, most people speak English or Afrikaans. Afrikaans was developed by the early Dutch settlers.

The rest of the continent—more than one-third of the people—speak one of the hundreds of Black African languages. For example, about 300 Bantu languages are used in central, eastern, and southern Africa, of which Swahili is the most widely spoken. One unusual group of lan-

Buildings Made of Mud

The most common building material in the world is not wood but mud, especially in Africa, where trees are scarce in many areas. The largest mud building in the world today is the Great Mosque (an Islamic temple) in Djenne, Mali, in western Africa. Built in 1907 in one of Africa's oldest cities, the mosque must be replastered with mud every spring.

guages, Khoisan, is often called a "click" language because its speakers use clicking sounds to convey certain words.

What is a lingua franca?

A lingua franca is a common second language used to communicate among people who speak different native languages. The Swahili language is a lingua franca. Although Swahili is an African tongue, it has many Arabic words because much Arabic trade once took place on Africa's eastern coast. English is also a lingua franca in Africa.

What religions are practiced in Africa?

About one-fourth of all Africans practice local, traditional religions, of which there are several hundred. In northern Africa, most people practice Islam. About 130 million Africans are Christians.

Where is the world's largest church?

Built in 1989, the Basilica of Our Lady of Peace can hold 18,000 people. It is located in Yamoussoukro, the capital of Côte d'Ivoire, a country on Africa's west coast. The church was built in just three years. Its dome rises higher than the dome of St. Peter's Basilica in Rome.

How did the country called Côte d'Ivoire, or the Ivory Coast, get its name?

Elephants, with their ivory tusks, were once numerous in the region. It was named by the French in the

In 1913, seven European countries— Belgium, France, Germany, Great Britain, Italy, Portugal, and Spain—controlled every part of Africa except for two countries: Liberia and Ethiopia.

The mosque in Djenne, Mali, was constructed in 1907 of mud, a common building material in Africa. Every spring a great festival is held, and participants gather to trade, worship, and replaster their mosque, the largest mud building in the world.

1400s, when they began trading in ivory there. Its official name is now the Republic of Côte d'Ivoire.

Today, Côte d'Ivoire is one of the richest countries in Africa. About the size of New Mexico, it's one of the world's largest producers and exporters of coffee, cocoa beans, and palm oil.

Is there really such a place as Timbuktu?

Yes, Timbuktu is the capital city of Mali, a country on the southern edge of the Sahara Desert. The word itself means "faraway place" in several African languages. It became an important trade center around 1300 for items such as gold, ivory, and slaves. Five hundred years ago, Timbuktu was home to 1 million people, but today only about 20,000 live there. Mali was a French colony until 1960.

Why are most African nations so poor?

Africa is the least developed continent in the world, with the exception of Antarctica. Most of its people are uneducated and must farm for a living. But farming is not easy in countries with poor soils, frequent floods and droughts, erratic weather, frequent insect invasions, and primitive tools. Most farmers grow only enough food to support their own families because they can't afford to buy fertilizers or invest in irrigation systems.

Why can't other nations send enough food to African countries during times of famine?

The rest of the world produces enough food to feed Africa, but the problem is that it's often difficult or impossible to get it to the people who need it. Roads are very bad in most of Africa and railroads and airports are few and far between. In addition, most countries are quite large and distances are great, and the food spoils on the way. War and politics also often keep food from reaching starving people.

What products does Africa export to the rest of the world?

In agriculture, Africa produces most of the world's yams, cocoa beans, and cassava. It is the leading producer of gold, copper, and diamonds. The country of South Africa is the world's largest producer of gold.

How much of Africa is covered by forests?

Less than one-fifth of the continent is forested—primarily tropical rain forests. Savannas, or grasslands, cover two-fifths of Africa (the Serengeti Plain is one example). Deserts cover the remaining two-fifths of the continent.

Why are Africa's rain forests disappearing at such an alarming rate?

As the population grows, forests are being cleared so that farmers can plant more crops. Trees are also being cut down for use as firewood. Wood is the primary source of fuel in Africa.

Making a phone call in most of Africa is not nearly as easy as it is in the United States. Africa has about 7 million phones, and half of those are in the country of South Africa. In comparison, there are nearly 200 million phones in the United States.

The Great Rift Valley in eastern Africa was formed by the movement of two tectonic plates drifting away from each other. As the plates continue to separate, some geologists predict the land on the eastern side of the rift will separate from the continent of Africa entirely.

What makes the Great Rift Valley so unusual?

The Great Rift Valley is the longest rift in the world. It was formed when tectonic forces created giant cracks in the earth's crust and began spreading apart. It is 3,750 miles (6000 km) long and more than 50 miles (80 km) wide at some points.

The Great Rift Valley begins in Jordan, near Syria in southwestern Asia, and extends across Kenya, Tanzania, and Malawi to Mozambique in eastern Africa. Many volcanic mountains surround the valley, including Africa's tallest peak, Mount Kilimanjaro.

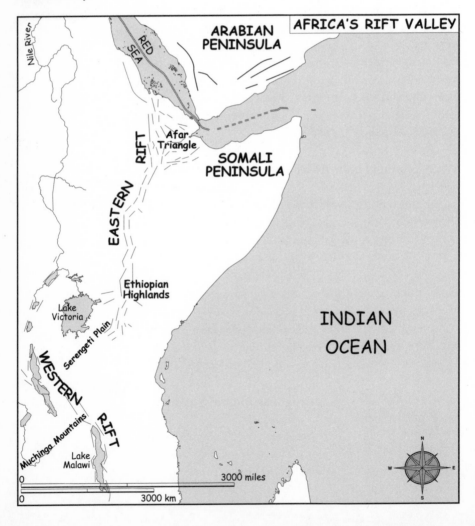

AFRICA'S RIFT VALLEY

The Great Rift Valley is still pulling apart a few inches every hundred years, and some geologists predict that part of East Africa will one day split away from the rest of the continent.

Where is Africa's largest lake?

Lake Victoria, in the countries of Kenya, Tanzania, and Uganda, is the continent's largest lake and the world's second largest freshwater lake, after Lake Superior on the U.S.-Canadian border. Lake Victoria covers 26,828 square miles (69,484 sq km)—about the same area as the country of Ireland.

Lake Tanganyika, also in eastern Africa and touching the countries of Zaire, Tanzania, and Zambia, is the *longest* freshwater lake in the world. It is 420 miles (680 km) long and more than 4,700 feet (1,430 m) deep. Like many other long, deep lakes in this part of Africa, it was formed in the bottoms of rift valleys.

Where are the Victoria Falls?

The Victoria Falls are on the Zambezi River, which forms the border between Zambia and Zimbabwe in southern Africa. The falls form the world's largest sheet of falling water. They are 1 mile (1.6 km) wide and drop 420 feet (128 m) into a narrow chasm. People can sometimes hear the roar of the falls from as far as 25 miles (40 km) away. They were discovered in 1855 by the British explorer David Livingstone, who named them after Queen Victoria.

Is it true that the Okavango River does not flow into the sea?

That's right. It ends by flowing into an inland swamp.

Do many people drive cars in Africa?

Only 2 people out of 100 in Africa own a car. Most roads are unpaved, making driving difficult or impossible during rainy periods. The most dangerous country in the world in which to drive is Malawi, in southeastern Africa.

Mount Kilimanjaro rises 19,340 feet (5,895 m) above sea level in Tanzania in eastern Africa, near the Equator. Even in this tropical climate, the mountains here are so high that they are covered with snow most of the year.

Drivers and their passengers are 30 times more likely to be injured in an accident there than in the United States.

Where is the Maghreb region of Africa?

The Maghreb—an Arabic word meaning "west"—refers to northwestern Africa. This part of the continent was conquered by the Arabs in the seventh century and remains Arabic in culture and religion today. It borders on the Atlantic Ocean and the Mediterranean Sea.

Countries in this region are Morocco, Algeria, Tunisia, and Libya and the area known as Western Sahara, which is trying to gain its independence from Morocco.

Where in Africa did most of the slave trade take place?

A total of about 10 to 12 million Africans were brought by Europeans to North and South America beginning in the 1500s. Most North American slaves came from west Africa, including the area of today's countries of Gambia, Ghana, the Ivory Coast, Nigeria, Senegal, and Sierra Leone. Many South American slaves came from Angola and Mozambique.

The Islamic slave trade began much earlier and spanned 12 centuries. During that period, Arabic people shipped unknown millions of Africans from eastern Africa to Spain, the Middle East, and India.

Cameroon's Killer Lakes

Lake Nios, in the African country of Cameroon, killed about 1,800 people in 1986 when it exploded and sent vast amounts of carbon dioxide and sulfuric acid gases into the air. The eruption occurred because the lake sits on top of a volcanic vent. The gases slowly seeped into the lake, and eventually built up to the point where they caused the lake to turn over in an explosive burst.

A similar explosion at nearby Lake Monoun killed 37 people two years earlier. French scientists are working on a project they hope will prevent these gases from building up in the future.

What makes Liberia unique among African countries?

Liberia was Africa's first independent country. It was founded by freed American slaves and settled beginning in the 1800s, with the financial help of private citizens in the United States. Its capital, Monrovia, was named for U.S. president James Monroe. Today its tropical rain forests provide the raw material for the country's large rubber industry.

The small west African country of Guinea-Bissau is the only country in the world that allows 15-year-olds to vote.

Do people still hunt wild animals in Kenya?

Kenya, on the east coast of Africa along the Equator, has an amazing variety of wild animals—antelope, buffaloes, crocodiles, elephants, giraffes, hippopotamuses, leopards, lions, rhinoceroses, and zebras, to name a few—but hunting has been illegal in Kenya since 1977. Half a million tourists visit Kenya's many national parks and game reserves each year on photographic safaris, though.

Why do two African countries have the same name: Congo?

There are two Congos, separated by the Congo River, and they are quite different countries. The Republic of the Congo is the smaller of the two. It was once a French colony and is now a democracy. Its eastern border touches the Democratic Republic of the Congo, which was called Zaire until a military dictatorship took over the country in 1997.

Zaire was once known as the Belgian Congo. It was a colony of Belgium from 1908 until it gained independence in 1960. It's interesting to note that many countries with the words "Democratic Republic of" in their names are dictatorships, not democracies.

Was Madagascar once part of Africa?

Madagascar, officially known as the Malagasy Republic, is the world's fourth largest island. At 1,000 miles (1,610 km) long, it has about the same land area as Texas. The island was once part of the African continent but broke away into the Indian Ocean about 160 million years ago.

Scientists estimate that about 150,000 of the 200,000 living things on Madagascar are not found anywhere else in the world.

Land of the Dodo Bird

Mauritius, a small island nation in the Indian Ocean east of Madagascar, was once home to the flightless dodo bird, which Dutch settlers hunted to extinction in the 1600s.

Madagascar is known for its amazing number and variety of plants and animals, including half the world's chameleon species. Its major export is vanilla, which comes from the beans of an orchid plant.

The people, who are a mix of African and Malay-Indonesian descent, are called Malagasy and speak a language of the same name.

Why is Africa called the "birthplace of the human race"?

Because scientists have found fossilized bones of human ancestors in eastern and southern Africa that are the oldest of any in the world. They believe that humans gradually moved out of Africa to populate the rest of the world.

Where is Olduvai Gorge, where fossilized bones of early human ancestors were found?

Olduvai Gorge is in Tanzania's Serengeti National Park, where evidence of early humans dates back about 2 million years. Other marvels in Tanzania include Mount Kilimanjaro, Lake Victoria (Africa's largest lake), and Lake

Ngorongoro Crater

One of Tanzania's most interesting places is Ngorongoro, a huge volcanic crater, or caldera. Probably the largest unbroken caldera in the world, Ngorongoro is 20 miles (32 km) wide and nearly 2,000 feet (600 m) deep. More than 30,000 animals live within the crater, including black rhinos, buffaloes, elephants, flamingos, leopards, lions, and zebras.

Tanganyika (the world's longest and second deepest lake). All of these sights are in the region of Africa's Great Rift Valley.

What makes the Namib Desert, in Namibia, so unusual?

The barren red sand desert known as Namib is the richest source of diamonds in the world. The desert stretches along Africa's southwestern coast for 1,300 miles (2,093 km). When the cold waters of the South Atlantic Ocean collide with the hot dry air of the African desert, huge amounts of fog blanket the coastal areas. But even with all that moisture, the Namib receives only 0.5 inch (1.27 cm) of rain each year.

The Namib Desert is about 55 million years old, making it one of the world's oldest deserts.

Why is South Africa the richest country in Africa?

Today, South Africa is the most industrialized country on the continent. It grew rich because Dutch colonists discovered gold and diamonds there in the late 1800s. South Africa still supplies about one-third of the world's gold yearly, mining more gold than any other country.

Other types of mining are important to the South African economy; in fact, almost every useful mineral on the earth, except for oil, is found there.

What is apartheid?

Apartheid is an Afrikaans word meaning "separateness," in this case referring to the strict separation of the black and white races. Beginning in the late 1940s, apartheid was the official policy of the South African government.

Under this policy, only white people, who formed just 15 percent of the population, had political and economic power. South African blacks were denied many rights, including the right to vote. The practice of apartheid was stopped in 1994. That year, Nelson Mandela, the country's first black leader, was elected president. Progress has been made in ensuring equality for all races, but discrimination remains a problem in South Africa.

What countries make up the world region called Oceania?
◆ What do the terms CHAPTER 7 Melanesia, and Polynesia mean? ◆ Which countries lie in the region geographers call Oceania? ◆ Where is Papua New Guinea? ◆ What are the smallest countries in Oceania? ◆ How far away is Australia from the United States? ◆ Australia and the United Kingdom? ◆ Is it true that Australia was originally a British prison colony? ◆ Do many immigrants live in Australia? ◆ How does Australia compare with the United States? ◆ Where is the outback? ◆ Did people live in Australia before the Europeans came in the 1700s? ◆ Is the island of Tasmania part of Australia? ◆ Is there really an animal called

OCEANIA AND ANTARCTICA

What countries make up the world region called Oceania?

There are 13 independent countries in Oceania: Federated States of Micronesia, Fiji, Kiribati, the Marshall Islands, Nauru, New Zealand, Palau, Papua New Guinea, Samoa, Solomon Islands, Tonga, Tuvalu, and Vanuatu. Several other islands are territories of other countries, including the U.S. state of Hawaii. Australia is sometimes considered part of Oceania, but not always.

All these nations consist of large groups of beautiful Pacific islands. Some geographers estimate that, in all, there may be 20,000 to 30,000 islands. Some are no more than rocks jutting out in the ocean, while others are home to thousands of people. If you were to add up all the land area of the islands in Oceania, the amount would come to less than the state of Alaska. In fact, the land area of Papua New Guinea and the two large islands of New Zealand account for 80 percent of all the land area in Oceania.

What do the terms Micronesia, Melanesia, and Polynesia mean?

These names refer to geographic divisions of Oceania. Micronesia refers to the more than 2,000 small islands that mostly lie north of the Equator. They include the Gilbert

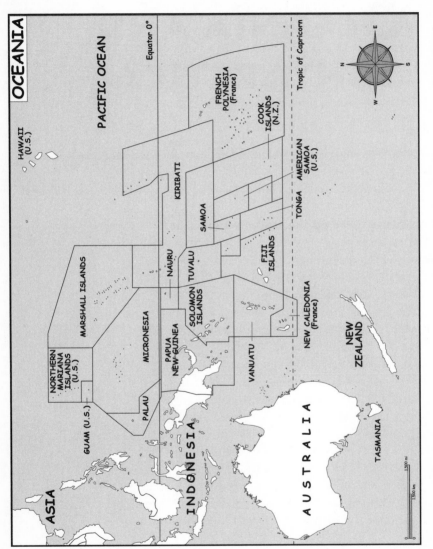

Australia is the world's smallest continent. It shares the southern Pacific Ocean with the 1,500 islands of Melanesia and the 5,000-mile stretch of ocean that contains the islands of Polynesia. Together with Micronesia, lying north of the Equator, these three groups of islands plus New Zealand are known as Oceania.

Islands, Guam, the Mariana Islands, the Marshall Islands, and Nauru.

The 1,500 islands of Melanesia lie south of the Equator and include Fiji, New Caledonia, Papua New Guinea, the Solomon Islands, and Vanuatu.

Polynesia is the largest of the three groups. It covers a huge area of the South Pacific, from the Midway Islands to New Zealand, a distance of more than 5,000 miles (8,000 km).

Where is Papua New Guinea?

Papua New Guinea is a country that occupies more than half the island of New Guinea, about 100 miles north of Australia. (The country of Indonesia occupies the western end of the island.) This island was formed when part of the continent of Australia broke away millions of years ago.

Papua New Guinea gained its independence from the European country of Austria in 1975. The country is a lush tropical paradise covered with mountains, forests, and woodland. It has 9,000 species of plants, 250 species of mammals, and 700 species of birds. Almost 5 million people live there, and more than 700 different languages are spoken. Many of those languages have only a few hundred speakers, though. English is the official language, but few people outside of government and business speak it.

What are the smallest countries in Oceania?

Tuvalu and Nauru are the two smallest. Nauru has 11,000 people living on an 8-square-mile (21 sq km) island. Tuvalu has 12,000 citizens living on nine coral atolls that together total only 10 square miles (26 sq km) of land area, but they stretch out over 360 miles of ocean.

How far away is Australia from the United States?

Australia is about 7,000 miles southwest from North America, lying between the South Pacific Ocean and the Indian Ocean. A commercial airplane flight to Australia's largest city, Sydney, takes more than 14 hours nonstop from Los Angeles.

Australia is the only country that is also a continent. It is the world's smallest and flattest continent, and it is the world's sixth largest country in land area.

*The name
Australia comes
from the Latin
word australis,
meaning
southern.*

Is Australia part of the United Kingdom?

No, not since 1901, when its six colonies formed the Commonwealth of Australia. Like New Zealand, it is a member of the Commonwealth of Nations, an organization of countries that were once part of the United Kingdom.

Queen Elizabeth II remains queen of Australia, even though her role is mainly symbolic. Many Australians would like to see Australia change its government from the present form of a constitutional monarchy, with a prime minister, to that of a republic, with a president.

Is it true that Australia was originally a British prison colony?

Yes, beginning in the late 1700s, the United Kingdom sent convicted criminals to this faraway territory. Until that time, the British had been sending convicts to their American colonies, but the American Revolution put an end to that practice. Over a period of 80 years, some 160,000 convicts were put on ships to Australia. But once the word got out in the 1850s that Australia's hills were rich with gold, thousands of British immigrants began to move there on their own.

Do many immigrants live in Australia?

One of every five people living in Australia today was born in another country. Australia's population has more than doubled since 1950, and most of that increase has been due to immigration. In recent years, most people immigrating to Australia have come from Asian countries.

How does Australia compare with the United States?

Australia has about 19 million people—almost as many people as live in New York State. In land area, it is about the size of the United States minus Alaska. Most Australians—about 80 percent of them—live in the southeastern part of the country, mostly in the cities and suburbs of Sydney, Melbourne, and Canberra, the capital.

The huge interior of Australia, known as the outback, is mostly flat and dry and is sparsely populated. Australia

The World's Longest, Straightest Railway

Often called "the long straight," Australia's transcontinental railroad, known as the Indian Pacific, includes the longest straight stretch of railway in the world. The straight part of the track, between Nurina and Loongana, in Western Australia, is 296 miles (477 km) long. The Indian Pacific railway is the second longest railway line in the world. It stretches for nearly 2,500 miles (4,025 km) across Australia, connecting Perth on the Indian Ocean with Sydney on the Pacific Ocean. The trip takes about three days.

The world's longest railway is the Trans-Siberian Express, which connects Moscow and Vladivostok and crosses 5,778 miles (9,245 km) in nine days.

---

has six states, which were once British colonies: New South Wales, Queensland, South Australia, Tasmania, Victoria, and Western Australia.

Where is the outback?

The huge central interior of the Australian continent is made up of desert land known as the outback. It is hot, dry, and sparsely populated.

Almost in the middle of the outback is the world's largest monolith, the famous red rock called Uluru, also known as Ayers Rock. It is 2.2 miles (3.6 km) long and 1,141 feet (348 m) high. Uluru is sacred to the Aboriginal people who have long lived in the area.

Uluru was once part of a large mountain range that began forming more than 500 million years ago. The mountain range eroded over the years, leaving Uluru and several smaller mountain ranges behind.

Australia is home to the world's only egg-laying mammals: the platypus and the echidna.

Did people live in Australia before the Europeans came in the 1700s?

Australia was home to Aborigines and Torres Strait Islanders for at least 65,000 years before Europeans settled the continent. Their plight has been similar to that of the native people in the Americas, with thousands either killed in fights with the early settlers or indirectly by the diseases the settlers introduced.

Since then, the native people of Australia have suffered a decline in population, racial discrimination, and loss of their ancient cultures. The Australian government is working to improve economic conditions for these native people and ensure their representation in national affairs.

Is the island of Tasmania part of Australia?

Yes, it is one of its six states. Until about 12,000 years ago it was connected to Australia's mainland. Then, rising sea waters resulting from the end of the last ice age covered the land bridge that connected Tasmania to Australia. Tasmania lies about 130 miles (209 km) south of the mainland.

Is there really an animal called the Tasmanian devil?

Yes, and it lives in Tasmania, a large island off the southern coast of Australia. Scientists think it became extinct on the Australian mainland about 600 years ago. The Tasmanian devil is nocturnal and about the size of a small, thick-set dog. It is covered with black fur, sometimes with a few white markings. It is the world's largest surviving carnivorous marsupial. Early settlers to the area gave it its name because of its hair-raising screeches and bad temper.

Why does Australia have so many unusual native animals, such as kangaroos and wombats?

Australia became a separate continent more than 200 million years ago—plenty of time for animals to develop in a distinctively different way from animals on other continents. More than 120 species of marsupials—mammals that give birth to very immature babies who continue to develop in their mothers' pouches—live in Australia today. These include kangaroos, koalas, Tasmanian devils, wallabies, and wombats.

What's so special about the Great Barrier Reef in Australia?

The Great Barrier Reef is the largest collection of coral reefs in the world. Hundreds of broken chains of coral reefs extend for about 1,250 miles (2,012 km) off the northeastern coast of Australia.

The Great Barrier Reef is home to hundreds of species of fish and other sea life, in addition to 350 species of living corals, the small plantlike animals that give the reefs their colorful appearance. The limestone formations that shape the reefs are made up of the calcified skeletons of the coral organisms.

In recent years, the health of the Great Barrier Reef has been threatened by human actions, such as tourism, pollution, and oil exploration, as well as by natural menaces such as cyclones and invasions of crown-of-thorns starfish, which feed on living corals.

Is New Zealand close to Australia?

Not really—New Zealand lies about 1,000 miles (1,610 km) southeast of Australia, across the Tasman Sea. Most of the country consists of two main islands—the North and the South—which together extend for about 1,000 miles (1,610 km).

How did New Zealand get its name?

New Zealand was discovered by Abel Tasman, a Dutch sea captain, in 1642. When his men tried to land, they were killed by the Maori, New Zealand's native people. Later, the Dutch gave the islands the name of Nieuw Zeeland after the province of Zeeland in the Netherlands.

Who are the Maori people?

The Maori first came to New Zealand about a thousand years ago from the Polynesian islands northeast of the country, possibly the Cook Islands, the Society Islands, or the Marquesas. Today, the Maori make up about 14 percent of New Zealand's population, and they still speak their native language. Most New Zealanders are descendants of settlers who arrived from Great Britain in the 1800s.

What makes New Zealand unique?

New Zealand is located in the Southern Hemisphere about halfway between the Equator and Antarctica. It sits on top of two tectonic plates, whose movement has

New Zealand has many more sheep than people— some 58 million sheep outnumber the 3.8 million human residents by more than 15 to 1.

New Zealand was the first country in the world to give women the right to vote. That was in 1893.

resulted in the South Island's magnificent mountains known as the Southern Alps. Mount Cook is the tallest of these craggy mountains, at 12,310 feet (3,753 m). In an area about the size of California, visitors can experience a range of landforms, from glaciers to rain forests.

New Zealand has been a separate microcontinent for 80 million years, plenty of time for diverse forms of life to evolve there. About 90 percent of its insects and 80 percent of its trees, ferns, and flowering plants are not found anywhere else on the earth. New Zealand also has 60 unique reptile species—but not a single snake.

New Zealand is home to one of the world's largest and heaviest insects, the giant weta. Wetas are flightless, grasshopper-like insects that can weigh twice as much as a small mouse.

New Zealand's only native land mammals are two species of bats. All other mammals there were brought from somewhere else.

Several species of flightless birds are unique to New Zealand. Because they had no natural enemies, these birds could walk freely on the ground and never needed to use their wings. The best known is the kiwi, the New Zealand national emblem. This shy, nocturnal bird has nostrils at the end of its beak.

Which continent is the highest, the driest, and the coldest?

Antarctica, the land that surrounds the South Pole, is even colder than the North Pole. It rarely snows in the interior because the air is so dry due to the continent's high elevation. Along the coasts, rain and snowfall average about 24 inches (61 cm) a year.

Antarctica is also the highest continent in average elevation above sea level. This is because it is covered by a huge layer of ice—about 7,100 feet (2,200 m) thick. Beneath all that ice is a land that looks much like other continents, with mountains, valleys, and plains. Millions of years ago, Antarctica was ice-free.

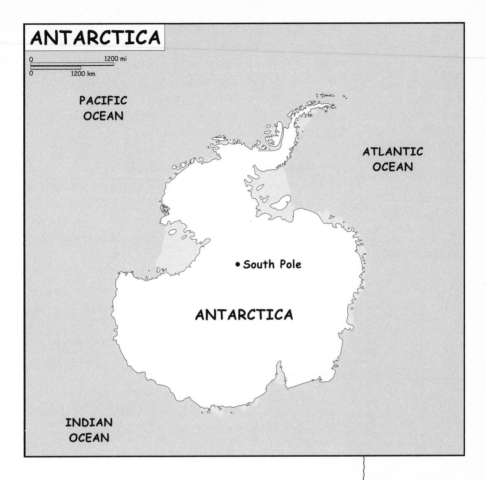

ANTARCTICA

0 ————— 1200 mi
0 ——— 1200 km

PACIFIC
OCEAN

ATLANTIC
OCEAN

• South Pole

ANTARCTICA

INDIAN
OCEAN

What would happen if the Antarctic ice sheet melted?

If the Antarctic ice sheet melted, the sea level around the world would rise about 220 feet (67 m)—the height of a 20-story building. About 90 percent of the world's ice is held in that ice sheet.

Is Antarctica a country?

No. Although several countries have claimed parts of the continent of Antarctica, the United States and a few other countries have not recognized those claims. Twenty-

Antarctica is larger in area than Europe, Australia, and the United States, but it has the smallest population of any continent—in fact, no one lives there permanently .

Many countries have claimed parts of Antarctica, but the nations of the world disagree about some of these claims. For example, as this map shows, Great Britain, Argentina, and Chile all claim part of the same territory, as do Australia and New Zealand.

six countries have signed the Antarctic Treaty, which states that countries must use Antarctica for peaceful purposes only. Many countries would like to claim parts of Antarctica because they believe it contains large oil and mineral resources. Currently, the treaty bans mineral and oil exploration. It also keeps countries from officially settling their claims to land there.

How cold does it get in Antarctica?

The world's lowest recorded temperature was at Vostok Station on July 21, 1983, when the thermometer dropped to –128.6° F (–89.2° C). Year-round in Antarctica, the temperature rarely rises above freezing. It is dark there for six months a year.

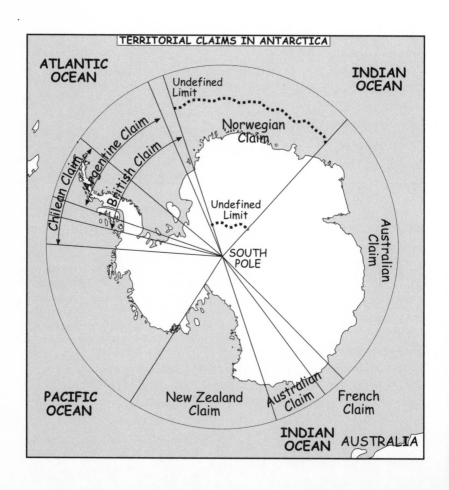

Do any plants or animals live in Antarctica?

Yes, those that can survive the cold, dry climate, such as mosses, lichens, and algae. Only a few small insects can live there, and then only in the coastal areas.

Many more animals spend summers in the waters that surround the continent, including penguins, seals, whales, and several kinds of birds. Krill, squid, and many kinds of fish also live in the Antarctic Ocean. Fossil remains of dinosaurs, small mammals, and trees have been found in Antarctica. They lived millions of years ago, before Antarctica was as cold as it is today.

Do any people live in Antarctica?

Yes, several countries have set up about 30 scientific research stations there. One of the largest is the U.S.'s McMurdo Station, where about 4,000 people live in the summer months. Most do not spend the winter months of June, July, and August there.

Who was the first person to reach the South Pole?

The Norwegian explorer Roald Amundsen arrived at the South Pole in December 1911.

Is Antarctica bigger than the United States?

Yes, it's 1.5 times larger. Antarctica covers about 5.4 million square miles (14 million sq km). It's also larger in area than either Europe or Australia.

WORLD COUNTRIES AND TERRITORIES LISTED ALPHABETICALLY

Afghanistan *Area:* 249,999 mi² (647,500 km²)
Capital: Kabul
Government: In transition
Population: 25,888,797
Languages: Pushtu, Afghan Persian, Turkic

Albania *Area:* 11,100 mi² (28,750 km²)
Capital: Tirana
Government: Republic
Population: 3,490,435
Languages: Albanian, Greek

Algeria *Area:* 919,590 mi² (2,381,740 km²)
Capital: Algiers
Government: Republic
Population: 31,193,917
Languages: Arabic, French, Berber dialects

Andorra *Area:* 174 mi² (450 km²)
Capital: Andorra la Vella
Government: Coprincipality of France and Spain
Population: 66,824
Languages: Catalan, French, Castilian

Angola *Area:* 481,351 mi² (1,246,700 km²)
Capital: Luanda
Government: Republic
Population: 10,145,267
Languages: Portuguese, Bantu dialects

Anguilla *Area:* 35 mi² (91 km²)
Capital: The Valley
Government: Dependent territory of United Kingdom
Population: 11,797
Language: English

Antarctica *Area:* 5,500,000 mi² (14,000,000 km²)
Capital: None
Government: Various nations—including Argentina, Australia, Chile, France, New Zealand, Norway, and United Kingdom—claim areas of the continent; Antarctic Treaty of 1959, signed by 42 nations, places these claims in abeyance and stipulates peaceful uses of Antarctica.

Population: No indigenous inhabitants; seasonal population of researchers averages about 4,000 in summer and 1,000 in winter.

Antigua and Barbuda
Area: 170 mi^2 (440 km^2)
Capital: Saint John's
Government: Parliamentary democracy affiliated with United Kingdom
Population: 66,464
Languages: English, local dialects

Argentina
Area: 1,068,296 mi^2 (2,766,890 km^2)
Capital: Buenos Aires
Government: Republic
Population: 36,955,182
Languages: Spanish, English, Italian, German, French

Armenia
Area: 11,306 mi^2 (29,283 km^2)
Capital: Yerevan
Government: Presidential republic
Population: 3,344,336
Languages: Armenian, Russian

Aruba
Area: 75 mi^2 (193 km^2)
Capital: Oranjestad
Government: Independent territory of the Netherlands
Population: 69,539
Languages: Dutch, Papiamento, Spanish, English

Australia
Area: 2,967,893 mi^2 (7,686,850 km^2)
Capital: Canberra
Government: Federal parliamentary state affiliated with Great Britain
Population: 19,164,620
Languages: English, native languages

Austria
Area: 32,374 mi^2 (83,850 km^2)
Capital: Vienna
Government: Federal republic
Population: 8,131,111
Language: German

Azerbaijan
Area: 33,400 mi^2 (86,506 km^2)
Capital: Baku
Government: Parliamentary republic
Population: 7,748,163
Languages: Azeri, Russian

Bahamas
Area: 5,382 mi^2 (13,940 km^2)
Capital: Nassau
Government: Independent commonwealth affiliated with United Kingdom
Population: 294,982
Languages: English, Creole

Bahrain
Area: 239 mi^2 (620 km^2)
Capital: Manama
Government: Monarchy
Population: 634,137
Languages: Arabic, English, Farsi, Urdu

Bangladesh   *Area:* 55,598 mi² (144,000 km²)
                    Capital: Dhaka
                    Government: Republic
                    Population: 129,194,224
                    Languages: Bangla, English

Barbados   *Area:* 166 mi² (460 km²)
                    Capital: Bridgetown
                    Government: Parliamentary democracy affiliated with United Kingdom
                    Population: 274,059
                    Language: English

Barbuda   *See* Antigua and Barbuda.

Belarus   *Area:* 80,200 mi² (207,718 km²)
                    Capital: Minsk
                    Government: Constitutional republic
                    Population: 10,366,719
                    Languages: Byelorussian, Russian

Belgium   *Area:* 11,784 mi² (30,520 km²)
                    Capital: Brussels
                    Government: Constitutional monarchy
                    Population: 10,241,506
                    Languages: Flemish, French

Belize   *Area:* 8,865 mi² (22,960 km²)
                    Capital: Belmopan
                    Government: Parliamentary democracy affiliated with United Kingdom
                    Population: 249,183
                    Languages: English, Spanish, Maya, Garifuna

Benin   *Area:* 43,483 mi² (112,620 km²)
                    Capital: Porto-Novo
                    Government: Multiparty democracy
                    Population: 6,395,919
                    Languages: French, Fon, Yoruba, tribal dialects

Bermuda   *Area:* 19 mi² (50 km²)
                    Capital: Hamilton
                    Government: Dependent territory of United Kingdom
                    Population: 63,022
                    Language: English

Bhutan   *Area:* 18,147 mi² (47,000 km²)
                    Capital: Thimphu
                    Government: Monarchy
                    Population: 2,005,222
                    Languages: Dzongkha, other Tibetan dialects, Nepalese dialects

Bolivia   *Area:* 424,162 mi² (1,098,580 km²)
                    Capitals: La Paz and Sucre
                    Government: Republic
                    Population: 8,152,620
                    Languages: Spanish, Quechua, Aymara

Bosnia and   *Area:* 19,741 mi² (51,129 km²)
Herzegovina   *Capital:* Sarajevo
                    Government: Republic

Population: 3,835,777
Languages: Serbo-Croatian

Botswana   *Area:* 231,803 mi² (600,370 km²)
Capital: Gaborone
Government: Parliamentary republic
Population: 1,576,470
Languages: English, Setswana

Brazil   *Area:* 3,286,472 mi² (8,511,970 km²)
Capital: Brasília
Government: Federal republic
Population: 172,860,370
Languages: Portuguese, Spanish, English, French

British Virgin Islands   *Area:* 58 mi² (150 km²)
Capital: Road Town
Government: Dependent territory of United Kingdom
Population: 20,353
Language: English

Brunei   *Area:* 2,228 mi² (5,770 km²)
Capital: Bandar Seri Begawan
Government: Constitutional sultanate
Population: 336,376
Languages: Malay, English, Chinese

Bulgaria   *Area:* 42,822 mi² (110,910 km²)
Capital: Sofia
Government: Emerging democracy
Population: 7,796,694
Language: Bulgarian

Burkina Faso   *Area:* 105,869 mi² (274,200 km²)
Capital: Ouagadougou
Government: Parliamentary republic
Population: 11,946,065
Languages: French, Sudanic tribal dialects

Burma   *See* Myanmar.

Burundi   *Area:* 10,745 mi² (27,830 km²)
Capital: Bujumbura
Government: Republic
Population: 6,054,714
Languages: Kirundi, French, Swahili

Cambodia   *Area:* 69,900 mi² (181,040 km²)
Capital: Phnom Penh
Government: Constitutional monarchy
Population: 12,212,306
Languages: Khmer, French

Cameroon   *Area:* 183,567 mi² (475,440 km²)
Capital: Yaoundé
Government: Unitary republic
Population: 15,421,937
Languages: English, French, African languages

Canada
Area: 3,851,788 mi² (9,976,140 km²)
Capital: Ottawa
Government: Confederation, with parliamentary democracy
Population: 31,278,097
Languages: English, French

Cape Verde
Area: 1,556 mi² (4,030 km²)
Capital: Praia
Government: Republic
Population: 401,343
Languages: Portuguese, Crioulo

Cayman Islands
Area: 100 mi² (260 km²)
Capital: George Town
Government: Dependent territory of United Kingdom
Population: 34,763
Language: English

Central African Republic
Area: 240,533 mi² (622,980 km²)
Capital: Bangui
Government: Military republic
Population: 3,512,751
Languages: French, Sangho, Arabic, Hunsa, Swahili

Chad
Area: 495,752 mi² (1,284,000 km²)
Capital: N'Djamena
Government: Republic
Population: 8,824,504
Languages: French, Arabic, Sara, Sango

Chile
Area: 292,258 mi² (756,950 km²)
Capital: Santiago
Government: Republic
Population: 15,152,797
Language: Spanish

China
Area: 3,705,386 mi² (9,596,960 km²)
Capital: Beijing
Government: Communist
Population: 1,261,832,482
Languages: Mandarin, Yue, Wu, Minbei, Minnan, Xiang, Gan, Hakka dialects

Christmas Island
Area: 52 mi² (135 km²)
Capital: The Settlement
Government: Territory of Australia
Population: 2,195
Language: English

Colombia
Area: 439,733 mi² (1,138,910 km²)
Capital: Bogotá
Government: Republic
Population: 39,685,655
Language: Spanish

Comoros
Area: 838 mi² (2,170 km²)
Capital: Moroni

Government: Independent republic
Population: 578,400
Languages: Arabic, French, Comorian

Congo, Democratic Republic of (formerly Zaire)
Area: 905,563 mi² (2,345,410 km²)
Capital: Kinshasa
Government: Republic
Population: 51,964,999
Languages: French, Lingala, Swahili, Kingwana, Kikongo, Tshiluba

Congo, Republic of the
Area: 132,046 mi² (342,000 km²)
Capital: Brazzaville
Government: Republic
Population: 2,830,961
Languages: French, Lingala, Kikongo

Cook Islands
Area: 93 mi² (240 km²)
Capital: Avarua
Government: Self-governing in association with New Zealand
Population: 19,989
Language: English

Costa Rica
Area: 19,730 mi² (51,100 km²)
Capital: San José
Government: Democratic republic
Population: 3,710,558
Languages: Spanish, English

Croatia
Area: 21,824 mi² (56,524 km²)
Capital: Zagreb
Government: Republic
Population: 4,282,216
Language: Serbo-Croatian

Cuba
Area: 42,803 mi² (110,860 km²)
Capital: Havana
Government: Communist
Population: 11,141,997
Language: Spanish

Cyprus
Area: 3,571 mi² (9,250 km²)
Capital: Nicosia
Government: Republic; northern part administered by Turkey
Population: 758,363
Languages: Greek, Turkish, English

Czech Republic
Area: 30,342 mi² (78,864 km²)
Capital: Prague
Government: Parliamentary democracy
Population: 10,272,179
Languages: Czech, Slovak

Denmark
Area: 16,629 mi² (43,070 km²)
Capital: Copenhagen
Government: Constitutional monarchy
Population: 5,336,394
Languages: Danish, Faroese, Greenlandic, German

Djibouti
Area: 8,494 mi² (22,000 km²)
Capital: Djibouti
Government: Republic
Population: 451,442
Languages: French, Arabic, Somali, Afar

Dominica
Area: 750 km² (290 mi²)
Capital: Roseau
Government: Parliamentary democracy
Population: 71,540
Languages: English, French patois

Dominican Republic
Area: 18,815 mi² (48,730 km²)
Capital: Santo Domingo
Government: Republic
Population: 8,442,533
Language: Spanish

Ecuador
Area: 109,483 mi² (283,560 km²)
Capital: Quito
Government: Republic
Population: 12,920,092
Languages: Spanish, Indian languages (especially Quechua)

Egypt
Area: 386,660 mi² (1,001,450 km²)
Capital: Cairo
Government: Republic
Population: 68,359,979
Languages: Arabic, English, French

El Salvador
Area: 8,124 mi² (21,040 km²)
Capital: San Salvador
Government: Republic
Population: 6,122,515
Languages: Spanish, Nahua

Equatorial Guinea
Area: 10,830 mi² (28,050 km²)
Capital: Malabo
Government: Republic
Population: 474,214
Languages: Spanish, French, Fang, Bubi, Ibo

Eritrea
Area: 45,754 mi² (123,300 km²)
Capital: Asmara
Government: In transition
Population: 4,135,933
Languages: Afar, Bilen, Kunama, Nara, Arabic, Tobedawi, Saho, Tigre, Tigrinya

Estonia
Area: 17,413 mi² (45,100 km²)
Capital: Tallinn
Government: Republic
Population: 1,431,471
Languages: Estonian, Russian

Ethiopia
Area: 437,600 mi² (1,133,380 km²)
Capital: Addis Ababa
Government: Constitutional republic

Population: 64,117,452
Languages: Amharic, Tigrinya, Orominga, Guaraginga, Somali, Arabic, English

Falkland Islands
Area: 4,699 mi² (12,170 km²)
Capital: Stanley
Government: Dependent territory of United Kingdom
Population: 2,805
Language: English

Faroe Islands
Area: 541 mi² (1,400 km²)
Capital: Tórshavn
Government: Self-governing overseas administrative division of Denmark
Population: 45,296
Languages: Faroese, Danish

Fiji
Area: 7,054 mi² (18,270 km²)
Capital: Suva
Government: Military republic
Population: 832,494
Languages: English, Fijian, Hindustani

Finland
Area: 130,127 mi² (337,030 km²)
Capital: Helsinki
Government: Republic
Population: 5,167,486
Languages: Finnish, Swedish, Lapp, Russian

France
Area: 211,208 mi² (547,030 km²)
Capital: Paris
Government: Republic
Population: 59,329,691
Languages: French, regional dialects

French Guiana
Area: 32,253 mi² (83,534 km²)
Capital: Cayenne
Government: Overseas department of France
Population: 172,605
Language: French

French Polynesia
Area: 1,544 mi² (4,000 km²)
Capital: Papeete
Government: Overseas territory of France
Population: 249,110
Languages: French, Tahitian

Gabon
Area: 103,347 mi² (267,670 km²)
Capital: Libreville
Government: Republic
Population: 1,208,436
Languages: French, Fang, Myene, Bateke, Bapounou/Eschira, Bandjabi

The Gambia
Area: 4,363 mi² (11,300 km²)
Capital: Banjul
Government: Republic
Population: 1,367,124
Languages: English, Mandinka, Wolof, Fula, local dialects

Georgia   *Area:* 26,911 mi^2 (69,699 km^2)
Capital: Tbilisi
Government: Republic
Population: 5,019,538
Languages: Georgian, Russian

Germany   *Area:* 137,803 mi^2 (356,910 km^2)
Capital: Berlin
Government: Federal republic
Population: 82,797,408
Language: German

Ghana   *Area:* 92,100 mi^2 (238,540 km^2)
Capital: Accra
Government: Republic
Population: 19,533,560
Languages: English, Akan, Moshi-Dagomba, Ewe, Ga-Adangbe

Gibraltar   *Area:* 2.5 mi^2 (6.5 km^2)
Capital: Gibraltar
Government: Dependent territory of United Kingdom
Population: 27,578
Languages: English, Spanish, Italian, Portuguese, Russian

Greece   *Area:* 50,942 mi^2 (131,940 km^2)
Capital: Athens
Government: Presidential parliamentary
Population: 10,601,527
Languages: Greek, English, French

Greenland   *Area:* 839,999 mi^2 (2,175,600 km^2)
Capital: Nuuk (Godthåb)
Government: Self-governing overseas administrative division of
   Denmark
Population: 56,309
Languages: Eskimo dialects, Danish

Grenada   *Area:* 131 mi^2 (340 km^2)
Capital: St. George's
Government: Parliamentary democracy affiliated with United Kingdom
Population: 89,312
Languages: English, French patois

Guadeloupe   *Area:* 687 mi^2 (1,780 km^2)
Capital: Basse-Terre
Government: Overseas department of France
Population: 426,493
Languages: French, Creole

Guatemala   *Area:* 42,042 mi^2 (108,890 km^2)
Capital: Guatemala City
Government: Republic
Population: 12,639,939
Languages: Spanish, Quiche, Cakchiquel, Kekchi, other Indian dialects

Guernsey   *Area:* 25 mi^2 (64 km^2)
Capital: St. Peter Port
Government: British crown dependency

Population: 65,386
Languages: English, French, Norman-French

Guinea
Area: 94,927 mi² (245,860 km²)
Capital: Conakry
Government: Republic
Population: 7,466,200
Languages: French, tribal languages

Guinea-Bissau
Area: 13,948 mi² (36,120 km²)
Capital: Bissau
Government: Republic
Population: 1,285,715
Languages: Portuguese, Criolo, African languages

Guyana
Area: 83,000 mi² (214,970 km²)
Capital: Georgetown
Government: Republic
Population: 697,286
Languages: English, Amerindian dialects

Haiti
Area: 10,714 mi² (27,750 km²)
Capital: Port-au-Prince
Government: Republic
Population: 6,867,995
Languages: French, Creole

Honduras
Area: 43,278 mi² (112,090 km²)
Capital: Tegucigalpa
Government: Republic
Population: 6,249,598
Languages: Spanish, Amerindian dialects

Hong Kong
Area: 416 mi² (1,077 km²)
Capital: None
Government: Special administrative region of China
Population: 7,120,000
Languages: Cantonese, English

Hungary
Area: 35,919 mi² (93,030 km²)
Capital: Budapest
Government: Republic
Population: 10,138,844
Language: Hungarian (Magyar)

Iceland
Area: 39,768 mi² (103,000 km²)
Capital: Reykjavík
Government: Republic
Population: 276,365
Languages: Icelandic

India
Area: 1,269,338 mi² (3,287,590 km²)
Capital: New Delhi
Government: Federal republic
Population: 1,014,003,817
Languages: Hindi, English, Bengali, Telugu, Marathi, Tamil, Urdu, Gujarati, Malayalan, Kannada, Oriya, Punjabi, Assamese, Kashmiri, Sindhi, Sanskrit, Hindustani

Indonesia *Area:* 735,272 mi² (1,904,570 km²)
Capital: Jakarta
Government: Republic
Population: 224,784,210
Languages: Bahasa Indonesian, Javanese, English, Dutch

Iran *Area:* 636,293 mi² (1,648,000 km²)
Capital: Teheran
Government: Theocratic republic
Population: 65,619,636
Languages: Farsi, Turk, Kurdish, Arabic, Luri, Baloch

Iraq *Area:* 167,923 mi² (434,920 km²)
Capital: Baghdad
Government: Republic
Population: 22,675,617
Languages: Arabic, Kurdish, Assyrian, Armenian

Ireland *Area:* 27,135 mi² (70,280 km²)
Capital: Dublin
Government: Republic
Population: 3,797,257
Languages: English, Irish (Gaelic)

Israel *Area:* (excluding occupied territories) 8,019 mi² (20,770 km²)
Capital: Jerusalem
Government: Parliamentary democracy
Population: 5,842,454 (excluding occupied territories)
Languages: Hebrew, Arabic, English
See also West Bank and Gaza Strip

Italy *Area:* 116,305 mi² (301,230 km²)
Capital: Rome
Government: Republic
Population: 57,634,827
Languages: Italian, German, French, Slovene

Ivory Coast *Area:* 124,502 mi² (322,460 km²)
Capital: Abidjan (also Yamoussoukro)
Government: Republic
Population: 15,980,950
Languages: French, Dioula, tribal languages

Jamaica *Area:* 4,243 mi² (10,990 km²)
Capital: Kingston
Government: Parliamentary democracy affiliated with the United Kingdom
Population: 2,652,689
Languages: English, Creole

Japan *Area:* 145,882 mi² (377,835 km²)
Capital: Tokyo
Government: Constitutional monarchy
Population: 126,549,976
Language: Japanese

Jersey *Area:* 45 mi² (117 km²)
Capital: Saint Helier

Government: British crown dependency
Population: 89,721
Languages: English, French, Norman-French

Jordan
Area: 35,475 mi^2 (91,880 km^2) (excluding West Bank)
Capital: Amman
Government: Constitutional monarchy
Population: 4,998,564 (excluding West Bank)
Languages: Arabic, English

Kazakhstan
Area: 1,049,200 mi^2 (2,717,428 km^2)
Capital: Astana
Government: Constitutional republic
Population: 16,733,227
Languages: Kazakh, Russian

Kenya
Area: 224,961 mi^2 (582,650 km^2)
Capital: Nairobi
Government: Republic
Population: 30,339,770
Languages: English, Swahili, local languages

Kiribati
Area: 274 mi^2 (710 km^2)
Capital: Tarawa
Government: Republic
Population: 91,985
Languages: English, Gilbertese

Korea, Democratic People's Republic of (North Korea)
Area: 46,540 mi^2 (120,540 km^2)
Capital: Pyongyang
Government: Communist
Population: 21,687,550
Language: Korean

Korea, Republic of (South Korea)
Area: 38,023 mi^2 (98,480 km^2)
Capital: Seoul
Government: Republic
Population: 47,470,969
Language: Korean

Kuwait
Area: 6,880 mi^2 (17,820 km^2)
Capital: Kuwait City
Government: Nominal constitutional monarchy
Population: 1,973,572
Languages: Arabic, English

Kyrgyzstan
Area: 76,642 mi^2 (198,509 km^2)
Capital: Bishkek
Government: Constitutional republic
Population: 4,685,230
Languages: Kirghiz, Russian

Laos
Area: 91,428 mi^2 (236,800 km^2)
Capital: Vientiane
Government: Communist
Population: 5,497,459
Languages: Lao, French, English

Latvia
Area: 24,595 mi² (63,701 km²)
Capital: Riga
Government: Republic
Population: 2,404,926
Languages: Lettish, Lithuanian, Russian

Lebanon
Area: 4,015 mi² (10,400 km²)
Capital: Beirut
Government: Republic
Population: 3,578,036
Languages: Arabic, French, Armenian, English

Lesotho
Area: 11,718 mi² (30,350 km²)
Capital: Maseru
Government: Modified constitutional monarchy
Population: 2,143,141
Languages: Sesotho, English, Zulu, Xhosa

Liberia
Area: 43,000 mi² (111,370 km²)
Capital: Monrovia
Government: Republic
Population: 3,164,156
Languages: English, Niger-Congo languages

Libya
Area: 679,358 mi² (1,759,540 km²)
Capital: Tripoli
Government: Military dictatorship
Population: 5,115,450
Languages: Arabic, Italian, English

Liechtenstein
Area: 62 mi² (160 km²)
Capital: Vaduz
Government: Constitutional monarchy
Population: 32,204
Languages: German, Alemannic

Lithuania
Area: 25,170 mi² (65,190 km²)
Capital: Vilnius
Government: Republic
Population: 3,620,756
Languages: Lithuanian, Polish, Russian

Luxembourg
Area: 998 mi² (2,586 km²)
Capital: Luxembourg
Government: Constitutional monarchy
Population: 437,389
Languages: Luxembourgish, German, French, English

Macau
Area: 6 mi² (16 km²)
Capital: Macau
Government: In 1999, became the Macau Special Administrative
  Region (SAR) of China
Population: 496,837
Languages: Portuguese, Cantonese

Macedonia
Area: 9,928 mi² (25,713 km²)
Capital: Skopje
Government: Republic

Population: 2,041,467
Languages: Macedonian, Albanian, Serbo-Croatian

Madagascar
Area: 226,656 mi² (587,040 km²)
Capital: Antananarivo
Government: Republic
Population: 15,506,472
Languages: French, Malagasy

Malawi
Area: 45,745 mi² (118,480 km²)
Capital: Lilongwe
Government: Constitutional republic
Population: 10,385,849
Languages: English, Chichewa, Tombuka

Malaysia
Area: 127,316 mi² (329,750 km²)
Capital: Kuala Lumpur
Government: Constitutional monarchy with hereditary rulers in peninsular states
Population: 21,793,293
Languages: Malay, English, Chinese dialects, Tamil, Hakka dialects, tribal languages

Maldives
Area: 116 mi² (300 km²)
Capital: Male
Government: Republic
Population: 301,475
Languages: Divehi, English

Mali
Area: 478,764 mi² (1,240,000 km²)
Capital: Bamako
Government: Republic
Population: 10,685,948
Languages: French, Bambara

Malta
Area: 124 mi² (320 km²)
Capital: Valletta
Government: Parliamentary democracy
Population: 391,670
Languages: Maltese, English

Man, Isle of
Area: 227 mi² (588 km²)
Capital: Douglas
Government: British crown dependency
Population: 73,112
Languages: English, Manx Gaelic

Martinique
Area: 425 mi² (1,100 km²)
Capital: Fort-de-France
Government: Overseas department of France
Population: 414,516
Languages: French, Creole patois

Mauritania
Area: 397,953 mi² (1,030,700 km²)
Capital: Nouakchott
Government: Republic
Population: 2,667,859
Languages: Hasaniya Arabic, French, Toucouleur, Fula, Sarakole, Wolof

Mauritius   *Area:* 718 mi² (1,860 km²)
Capital: Port Louis
Government: Parliamentary democracy affiliated with United Kingdom
Population: 1,179,368
Languages: English, Creole, French, Hindi, Urdu, Hakka, Bojpoori

Mayotte   *Area:* 145 mi² (375 km²)
Capital: Dzaoudzi
Government: Territorial collectivity of France
Population: 155,911
Languages: Mahorian, French

Mexico   *Area:* 761,602 mi² (1,972,550 km²)
Capital: Mexico City
Government: Federal republic
Population: 100,349,766
Languages: Spanish, Mayan dialects

Moldova   *Area:* 13,012 mi² (33,701 km²)
Capital: Kishinev
Government: Republic
Population: 4,430,654
Languages: Romanian, Russian

Monaco   *Area:* 0.7 mi² (1.9 km²)
Capital: Monaco
Government: Constitutional monarchy
Population: 31,693
Languages: French, English, Italian, Monegasque

Mongolia   *Area:* 604,247 mi² (1,565,000 km²)
Capital: Ulaanbaatar
Government: Republic
Population: 2,616,383
Languages: Khalkha Mongol, Turkic, Russian, Chinese

Montserrat   *Area:* 39 mi² (100 km²)
Capital: Plymouth
Government: Dependent territory of United Kingdom
Population: 6,409
Language: English

Morocco   *Area:* 172,413 mi² (446,550 km²)
Capital: Rabat
Government: Constitutional monarchy
Population: 30,122,350
Languages: Arabic, French, Berber dialects

Mozambique   *Area:* 309,633 mi² (801,950 km²)
Capital: Maputo
Government: Republic
Population: 19,104,696
Languages: Portuguese, indigenous languages

Myanmar   *Area:* 261,216 mi² (676,550 km²)
(formerly   *Capital:* Yangon (Rangoon)
Burma)   *Government:* Military
Population: 41,734,853
Languages: Burmese, ethnic languages

Namibia
Area: 318,258 mi² (824,290 km²)
Capital: Windhoek
Government: Republic
Population: 1,771,327
Languages: Afrikaans, German, English, indigenous languages

Nauru
Area: 8 mi² (20 km²)
Capital: Yaren
Government: Republic
Population: 11,845
Languages: Nauruan, English

Nepal
Area: 54,363 mi² (140,800 km²)
Capital: Kathmandu
Government: Constitutional monarchy
Population: 24,702,119
Languages: Nepali, local languages

The Netherlands
Area: 16,033 mi² (41,526 km²)
Capital: Amsterdam and The Hague
Government: Constitutional monarchy
Population: 15,892,237
Language: Dutch

Netherlands Antilles
Area: 313 mi² (800 km²)
Capital: Willemstad (on Curacao)
Government: Autonomous territory of The Netherlands
Population: 207,827
Languages: Dutch, Papiamento, English, Spanish

New Caledonia
Area: 7,359 mi² (19,060 km²)
Capital: Nouméa
Government: Overseas territory of France
Population: 201,816
Languages: French, Melanesian-Polynesian dialects

New Zealand
Area: 103,737 mi² (268,680 km²)
Capital: Wellington
Government: Parliamentary democracy affiliated with the United Kingdom
Population: 3,819,762
Languages: English, Maori

Nicaragua
Area: 49,998 mi² (129,494 km²)
Capital: Managua
Government: Republic
Population: 4,812,569
Languages: Spanish, English, Amerindian dialects

Niger
Area: 489,189 mi² (1,267,000 km²)
Capital: Niamey
Government: Republic (under military control)
Population: 10,075,571
Languages: French, Hausa, Djerma

Nigeria
Area: 356,668 mi² (923,770 km²)
Capital: Lagos
Government: Republic
Population: 123,337,822
Languages: English, Hausa, Yoruba, Ibo, Fulani

Niue
Area: 100 mi² (260 km²)
Capital: Alofi
Government: Self-governing territory affiliated with New Zealand
Population: 1,837
Languages: Polynesian (Tongan-Samoan dialect), English

Norfolk Island
Area: 13 mi² (36 km²)
Capital: Kingston
Government: Territory of Australia
Population: 2,285
Languages: English, Norfolk

Norway
Area: 125,181 mi² (324,220 km²)
Capital: Oslo
Government: Constitutional monarchy
Population: 4,481,162
Languages: Norwegian, Lapp, Finnish

Oman
Area: 82,031 mi² (212,460 km²)
Capital: Muscat
Government: Absolute monarchy
Population: 2,533,389
Languages: Arabic, English, Baluchi, Urdu

Pakistan
Area: 310,401 mi² (803,940 km²)
Capital: Islamabad
Government: Federal republic
Population: 141,553,775
Languages: Urdu, English, Punjabi, Sindhi, Pushtu, Baluchi

Palau
Area: 177 mi² (458 km²)
Capital: Koror
Population: 18,766
Government: Parliamentary republic
Languages: English, Palauan

Panama
Area: 30,193 mi² (78,200 km²)
Capital: Panama City
Government: Centralized republic
Population: 2,808,268
Languages: Spanish, English

Papua New Guinea
Area: 178,259 mi² (461,690 km²)
Capital: Port Moresby
Government: Parliamentary democracy affiliated with the United Kingdom
Population: 4,926,984
Languages: English, Motu, local dialects

Paraguay
Area: 157,046 mi² (406,750 km²)
Capital: Asunción
Government: Republic
Population: 5,585,828
Languages: Spanish, Guarani

Peru
Area: 496,223 mi² (1,285,220 km²)
Capital: Lima
Government: Republic
Population: 27,012,899
Languages: Spanish, Quechua, Aymara

Philippines *Area:* 115,830 mi² (300,000 km²)
Capital: Manila
Government: Republic
Population: 81,159,644
Languages: Philipino (Tagalog), English

Poland *Area:* 120,727 mi² (312,680 km²)
Capital: Warsaw
Government: Democratic state
Population: 36,646,023
Language: Polish

Portugal *Area:* 35,552 mi² (92,080 km²)
Capital: Lisbon
Government: Republic
Population: 10,048,232
Language: Portuguese

Qatar *Area:* 4,247 km² (11,000 km²)
Capital: Doha
Government: Traditional monarchy
Population: 744,483
Languages: Arabic, English

Réunion *Area:* 969 mi² (2,510 km²)
Capital: Saint-Denis
Government: Overseas department of France
Population: 720,934
Languages: French, Creole

Romania *Area:* 91,699 mi² (237,500 km²)
Capital: Bucharest
Government: Republic
Population: 22,411,121
Languages: Romanian, Hungarian, German

Russia *Area:* 6,592,800 mi² (17,075,352 km²)
Capital: Moscow
Government: Constitutional republic
Population: 146,001,176
Language: Russian

Rwanda *Area:* 10,170 mi² (26,340 km²)
Capital: Kigali
Government: Republic (under military control)
Population: 7,229,129
Languages: Kinyarwanda, French, Kiswahili, English

St. Helena *Area:* 47 mi² (122 km²)
Capital: Jamestown
Government: Dependent territory of United Kingdom
Population: 7,197
Language: English

St. Kitts and Nevis *Area:* 104 mi² (269 km²)
Capital: Basseterre
Government: Constitutional monarchy affiliated with United Kingdom
Population: 38,819
Language: English

St. Lucia   *Area:* 239 mi² (620 km²)
Capital: Castries
Government: Parliamentary democracy affiliated with United Kingdom
Population: 156,260
Languages: English, French patois

St. Pierre and   *Area:* 93 mi² (242 km²)
Miquelon   *Capital:* Saint-Pierre
Government: Territorial collectivity of France
Population: 6,896
Language: French

St. Vincent   *Area:* 131 mi² (340 km²)
and the   *Capital:* Kingstown
Grenadines   *Government:* Constitutional monarchy affiliated with United Kingdom
Population: 115,461
Languages: English, French patois

Samoa   *Area:* 1,104 mi² (2,860 km²)
Capital: Apia
Government: Constitutional monarchy
Population: 179,466
Languages: Samoan, English

San Marino   *Area:* 23 mi² (60 km²)
Capital: San Marino
Government: Republic
Population: 26,937
Language: Italian

São Tomé and   *Area:* 371 mi² (960 km²)
Principe   *Capital:* São Tomé and Principe
Government: Republic
Population: 159,883
Languages: Portuguese, Fang

Saudi Arabia   *Area:* 829,995 mi² (2,149,690 km²)
Capital: Riyadh
Government: Monarchy
Population: 22,023,506
Language: Arabic

Senegal   *Area:* 75,748 mi² (196,190 km²)
Capital: Dakar
Government: Republic
Population: 9,987,494
Languages: French, Wolof, Pulaar, Diola, Mandingo

Seychelles   *Area:* 176 mi² (455 km²)
Capital: Victoria
Government: Republic
Population: 79,326
Languages: English, French, Creole

Sierra Leone   *Area:* 27,699 mi² (71,740 km²)
Capital: Freetown
Government: Republic

Population: 5,232,624
Languages: English, Mende, Krio, Temne

Singapore
Area: 244 mi² (633 km²)
Capital: Singapore
Government: Republic
Population: 4,151,720
Languages: Chinese, Tamil, Malay, English

Slovakia
Area: 18,928 mi² (49,035 km²)
Capital: Bratislava
Government: Parliamentary democracy
Population: 5,407,956
Languages: Slovak, Hungarian

Slovenia
Area: 7,817 mi² (20,246 km²)
Capital: Ljubljana
Government: Republic
Population: 1,927,593
Languages: Slovene, Serbo-Croatian

Solomon Islands
Area: 10,985 mi² (28,450 km²)
Capital: Honiara
Government: Independent parliamentary state within British commonwealth
Population: 466,194
Languages: Melanesian, English, local dialects

Somalia
Area: 246,201 mi² (637,660 km²)
Capital: Mogadishu
Government: In transition
Population: 7,253,137
Languages: Somali, Arabic, Italian, English

South Africa
Area: 471,444 mi² (1,221,040 km²)
Capital: Pretoria, Cape Town, and Bloemfontein
Government: Republic
Population: 42,421,021
Languages: Afrikaans, English, Zulu, Xhosa, Tswana

Spain
Area: 194,884 mi² (504,750 km²)
Capital: Madrid
Government: Parliamentary monarchy
Population: 39,996,671
Languages: Castilian Spanish, Catalan, Galician, Basque

Sri Lanka
Area: 25,332 mi² (65,610 km²)
Capital: Colombo
Government: Republic
Population: 19,238,575
Languages: Sinhala, Tamil, English

Sudan
Area: 967,493 mi² (2,505,810 km²)
Capital: Khartoum
Government: Republic, military
Population: 35,079,814
Languages: Arabic, Nubian, Ta Bedawie, Nilotic and Nilo-Hamitic dialects, Sudanic dialects, English

Suriname   *Area:* 63,039 mi² (163,270 km²)
Capital: Paramaribo
Government: Republic
Population: 431,303
Languages: Dutch, English, Sranan Tongo, Javanese

Svalbard   *Area:* 23,597 mi² (62,049 km²)
Capital: Longyearbyen
Government: Territory of Norway
Population: 3,231
Languages: Russian, Norwegian

Swaziland   *Area:* 6,703 mi² (17,360 km²)
Capital: Mbabane
Government: Independent monarchy within British commonwealth
Population: 1,083,289
Languages: English, Swati

Sweden   *Area:* 173,729 mi² (449,960 km²)
Capital: Stockholm
Government: Constitutional monarchy
Population: 8,873,052
Languages: Swedish, Lapp, Finnish

Switzerland   *Area:* 15,942 mi² (41,290 km²)
Capital: Bern
Government: Federal republic
Population: 7,262,372
Languages: German, French, Italian, Romansch

Syria   *Area:* 71,498 mi² (185,180 km²)
Capital: Damascus
Government: Military republic
Population: 16,305,659
Languages: Arabic, Kurdish, Armenian, Aramaic, Circassian, French

Taiwan   *Area:* 13,892 mi² (35,980 km²)
Capital: Taipei
Government: Republic
Population: 22,191,087
Languages: Mandarin Chinese, Taiwanese and Hakka dialects

Tajikistan   *Area:* 54,019 mi² (139,909 km²)
Capital: Dushanbe
Government: Republic
Population: 6,440,732
Languages: Tadzhik, Russian

Tanzania   *Area:* 364,899 mi² (945,090 km²)
Capital: Dar es Salaam (scheduled to move to Dodoma, 2005)
Government: Republic
Population: 35,306,126
Languages: Swahili, English

Thailand   *Area:* 198,455 mi² (514,000 km²)
Capital: Bangkok
Government: Constitutional monarchy

Population: 61,230,874
Languages: Thai, English, local dialects

Togo　*Area:* 21,927 mi² (56,790 km²)
Capital: Lomé
Government: One-party republic
Population: 5,018,502
Languages: French, Ewe, Mina, Dagomba, Kabyè

Tokelau　*Area:* 4 mi² (10 km²)
Capital: None (various local government agencies)
Government: Territory of New Zealand
Population: 1,503
Languages: Tokelauan, English

Tonga　*Area:* 289 mi² (748 km²)
Capital: Nuku'alofa
Government: Constitutional monarchy
Population: 102,321
Languages: Tongan, English

Trinidad and Tobago　*Area:* 1,981 mi² (5,130 km²)
Capital: Port-of-Spain
Government: Parliamentary democracy
Population: 1,175,523
Languages: English, Hindi, French, Spanish

Tunisia　*Area:* 63,170 mi² (163,610 km²)
Capital: Tunis
Government: Republic
Population: 9,593,402
Languages: Arabic, French

Turkey　*Area:* 301,382 mi² (780,580 km²)
Capital: Ankara
Government: Republican parliamentary democracy
Population: 65,666,677
Languages: Turkish, Kurdish, Arabic

Turkmenistan　*Area:* 188,417 mi² (488,000 km²)
Capital: Ashkhabad
Government: Republic
Population: 4,518,268
Languages: Turkmen, Russian

Turks and Caicos Islands　*Area:* 193 mi² (500 km²)
Capital: Grand Turk (Cockburn Town)
Government: Dependent territory of the United Kingdom
Population: 17,502
Language: English

Tuvalu　*Area:* 10 mi² (26 km²)
Capital: Funafuti
Government: Democracy affiliated with the United Kingdom
Population: 10,838
Languages: Tuvaluan, English

Uganda
Area: 91,135 mi² (236,040 km²)
Capital: Kampala
Government: One-party republic
Population: 23,317,560
Languages: English, Luganda, Swahili, Bantu and Nilotic languages

Ukraine
Area: 233,100 mi² (603,729 km²)
Capital: Kiev
Government: Republic
Population: 49,153,027
Languages: Ukrainian, Russian

United Arab Emirates
Area: 32,278 mi² (83,600 km²)
Capital: Abu Dhabi
Government: Federation of seven emirates
Population: 2,369,153
Languages: Arabic, Farsi, English, Hindi, Urdu

United Kingdom
Area: 94,525 mi² (244,820 km²)
Capital: London
Government: Constitutional monarchy
Population: 59,508,382
Languages: English, Welsh, Scottish Gaelic

United States
Area: 3,717,796 mi² (9,629,046 km²)
Capital: Washington, D.C.
Government: Federal republic
Population: 275,562,673
Languages: English, Spanish

Uruguay
Area: 68,039 mi² (176,220 km²)
Capital: Montevideo
Government: Republic
Population: 3,334,074
Language: Spanish

Uzbekistan
Area: 172,700 mi² (447,293 km²)
Capital: Tashkent
Government: Republic
Population: 24,755,519
Languages: Uzbek, Russian

Vanuatu
Area: 5,699 mi² (14,760 km²)
Capital: Port-Vila
Government: Republic
Population: 189,618
Languages: English, French, Bislama

Vatican City
Area: 108.7 acres (0.438 km²)
Capital: Vatican City
Government: Independent papal state
Population: 870
Languages: Italian, Latin

Venezuela
Area: 352,143 mi² (912,050 km²)
Capital: Caracas
Government: Republic

Population: 23,542,649
Languages: Spanish, Amerindian dialects, Portuguese, Italian

Vietnam
Area: 127,243 mi² (329,560 km²)
Capital: Hanoi
Government: Communist
Population: 78,773,873
Languages: Vietnamese, French, Chinese, English, Khmer, tribal dialects

Wallis and Futuna
Area: 106 mi² (274 km²)
Capital: Mata-Utu
Government: Overseas territory of France
Population: 15,283
Languages: French, Wallisian

West Bank and Gaza Strip
Area: 2,410 mi² (6,240 km²)
Capital: None
Government: Israeli military rule
Population: 1,427,741 (excluding Israeli settlers)
Languages: Arabic, Hebrew, English

Western Sahara
Area: 1,097 mi² (2,860 km²)
Capital: None
Government: Moroccan administrative protectorate
Population: 222,631
Languages: Hassaniya Arabic, Moroccan Arabic

Yemen
Area: 203,849 mi² (527,970 km²)
Capital: Sanaa
Government: Republic
Population: 17,479,206
Language: Arabic

Yugoslavia, Federal Republic of
(Consists of Serbia, the largest republic of preindependence Yugoslavia, and Montenegro, the smallest republic—this country has not been recognized by the United States.)
Area: 39,449 mi² (102,173 km²)
Capital: Belgrade
Government: Federal republic
Population: 10,662,087
Languages: Serbo-Croatian, Hungarian (Vojvodina), Albanian (Kosovo), Montenegrin

Zambia
Area: 290,583 mi² (752,610 km²)
Capital: Lusaka
Government: Multiparty state
Population: 9,582,418
Languages: English, indigenous languages and dialects

Zimbabwe
Area: 150,803 mi² (390,580 km²)
Capital: Harare
Government: Parliamentary democracy
Population: 11,342,521
Languages: English, Shona, Sindebele

GLOSSARY

A
alluvial plain the area of silt, clay, sand, or gravel deposited by a stream
aquifer a porous rock mass or rock layer that stores and transmits groundwater
archipelago a group of islands spread across a large body of water
atoll a circular coral reef that encloses a small lagoon
avalanche a rapid slide or fall of snow, ice, rocks, and trees

B
barrier island a landform that is created when waves deposit sand parallel to
the shoreline

C
caldera the steep-sided circular depression that forms after the eruption of a
large volcano

D
delta the flat, low-lying area that forms when a river deposits sediment as it
enters a large body of standing water
desert a region that receives less than 10 inches of precipitation yearly
dialect a regional variation of a language, with differences in vocabulary,
accents, pronunciation, and syntax

E
earthquake magnitude the stress released by an earthquake at its focus
ecosystem a group of organisms and the environment in which they live
erosion any kind of removal of sediment, by the force of water, ice, or air

F
fjord a narrow, deep ocean valley that extends inland and partially fills a
glacial trough

G
greenhouse gases gases in the atmosphere that include water vapor, carbon
dioxide, ozone, nitrous oxide, and methane

green revolution the introduction of high-yield, high-protein crops beginning in the 1960s in Mexico, India, the Philippines, Indonesia, and elsewhere

gross national product the total of the value of the goods and services a country produces in one year

H

hurricane a rotating tropical storm that has winds of at least 74 mph (119 kph); called a *typhoon* in the western Pacific Ocean; called a *cyclone* when it forms in the Bay of Bengal and the northern Indian Ocean

L

lingua franca a common language used by a population that speaks one or more other languages

M

magma the molten rock that lies beneath the earth's surface

meteorology the science of the atmosphere

migration the movement of people who cross a boundary to set up a new residence

mineral an inorganic solid with a characteristic chemical composition and crystal structure

monsoon a seasonal change in the direction of the prevailing wind

moraine deposits of rock left behind by a glacier

N

nation a society of people who share the same language, religion, history, and symbols

nation-state a state (country) in which the homeland of a nation is the same as the territory of the state

natural disaster a natural event that adversely affects people; in the United States, the term is used when more than 100 people die or more than $1 million in damage occurs

O

ozone layer the layer of ozone gas in the atmosphere that protects life on the earth by absorbing the sun's ultraviolet rays

P

Pangaea the supposed supercontinent from which all the earth's continents may have formed

plain an extensive area of level, treeless country

plateau extensive elevated area bounded by a steep cliff

prime meridian the line of 0 degrees longitude that passes through Greenwich, England

R

racism discrimination of people on the basis of appearance

rain forest a densely wooded area usually found in tropical climates that have an annual rainfall of about 80 inches (200 cm) or more

resource a natural source of wealth or revenue to a society

Richter scale a logarithmic scale of numbers that represent the relative amount of energy released by an earthquake

rift a fault or fissure in the earth

ring of fire the arc of volcanoes that circles most of the Pacific Ocean

S

seismology the study of earthquakes

state an independent political unit that claims jurisdiction over a territory and the people who live in it; in this sense, means the same as *country*

subduction the process that forces the downbent edge of a crustal plate underneath another plate

T

tariff a surcharge imposed by a state on imports that increases their price in relation to domestic products; meant to discourage purchase of foreign products

tornado a violently rotating column of air that descends to the ground during thunderstorms

tsunami huge ocean waves resulting from the displacement of the seafloor during an earthquake, landslide, or volcanic eruption

W

weathering a process that causes rocks to disintegrate and soil to decompose

wetland an area of land that is covered by water and supports vegetation adapted to wet conditions

SELECTED BIBLIOGRAPHY

De Blij, Harm. *Harm de Blij's Geography Book*. New York: John Wiley & Sons, 1995.

Decker, Robert, and Barbara Decker. *Volcanoes*. New York: W. H. Freeman & Co., 1997.

Demko, George, with Jerome Agel and Eugene Boe. *Why in the World: Adventures in Geography*. New York: Doubleday, 1992.

Grillet, Donnat V. *Where on Earth?* New York: Prentice Hall, 1991.

Heritage, Andrew, ed. *DK World Atlas*. 2d ed. New York: Dorling Kindersley, 2000.

Hess, Darrel, and Tom L. McKnight. *Study Guide, Physical Geography: A Landscape Appreciation*. New York: Prentice Hall College Division, 1999.

The Houghton Mifflin Dictionary of Geography: Places and Peoples of the World. New York: Houghton Mifflin Company, 1997.

Levy, Matthys. *Earthquake Games: Earthquakes and Volcanoes Explained by Games and Experiments*. New York: Margaret McElderry, 1997.

Lutgens, Frederick K., and Edward J. Tarbuck. *The Atmosphere: An Introduction to Meteorology*. New York: Prentice Hall, 2000.

National Geographic Society. *Exploring Your World*. Washington, D.C.: National Geographic Society, 1993.

———. *National Geographic Desk Reference*. Washington, D.C.: National Geographic Society, 2000.

Pollock, Steve. *Eyewitness: Ecology*. New York: Dorling Kindersley, 2000.

Pope, Joyce. *The Children's Atlas of Natural Wonders*. Brookfield, Conn.: Millbrook Press, 1995.

Stefoff, Rebecca. *The Young Oxford Companion to Maps and Mapmaking*. New York: Oxford University Press, 1995.

Taylor, Barbara. *Maps and Mapping.* New York: Kingfisher Books, 1993.

Watt, Fiona, Jeremy Gower, and Chris Shields. *Earthquakes and Volcanoes.* Usborne Understanding Geography Series. Tulsa, Okla.: EDC Publications, 1994.

Wright, David, and Jill Wright. *Facts on File Children's Atlas.* Facts on File Atlas Series. New York: Checkmark Books, 2000.

Wyckof, Jerome. *Reading the Earth: Landforms in the Making.* Mahwah, N.J.: Adastra West, 1999.

THE NEW YORK PUBLIC LIBRARY'S RECOMMENDED READING LIST

Ayo, Yvonne. *Africa*. New York: Dorling Kindersley, 2000.

Carter, William E. *South America*. New York: Franklin Watts, 1983.

The DK Geography of the World. New York: Dorling Kindersley, 1996.

Gallant, Roy A. *The Peopling of Planet Earth: Human Population Growth through the Ages*. New York: Collier Macmillan, 1990.

Ganeri, Anita. *Religions Explained: A Beginner's Guide to World Faiths*. New York: Henry Holt and Company, 1997.

Hall, Michele, and Howard Hall. *Secrets of the Ocean Realm*. New York: Carroll & Graf, 1997.

Heinrichs, Ann. *Australia*. New York: Children's Press, 1998.

The Illustrated Guide to World Religions. New York: Oxford University Press, 1998.

McNeese, Tim. *The Great Wall of China*. San Diego: Lucent Books, 1997.

Pratt, Paula. *Maps: Plotting Places on the Globe*. San Diego: Lucent Books, 1995.

Queen, J. Allen. *The Princeton Review's Geography Smart Junior*. New York: Random House, 1996.

Sattler, Helen Roney. *Our Patchwork Planet: The Story of Plate Tectonics*. New York: Lothrop, Lee and Shepard Books, 1995.

Sayre, April Pulley. *Europe*. Brookfield, Conn.: Twenty-first Century Books, 1998.

———. *North America*. Brookfield, Conn.: Twenty-first Century Books, 1998.

Woods, Michael. *Science on Ice: Research in Antarctica*. Brookfield, Conn.: Millbrook Press, 1995.

INTERNET RESOURCES

www.cia.gov/cia/publications/factbook—The CIA World Factbook site provides up-to-date statistics and facts about all the world's countries.

www.geography.state.gov—The geographic learning site of the U.S. Department of State features information and news of international affairs for students by grade level.

www.loc.gov/rr/international—Click on the "Special International Guides" on this Library of Congress web page and then go to "Country Studies" for historical, social, economic, and political analyses of many of the world's countries.

www.nationalgeographic.com/kids—A special site just for kids by National Geographic, with games, quizzes, and articles, amazing facts, and cartoons.

www.ncdc.noaa.gov—The site of the U.S. National Climatic Data Center is the world's largest archive of weather information.

www.prb.org—The Population Reference Bureau, an educational organization specializing in population issues, has many facts and interesting articles about the world's people.

www.theodora.com/maps—Maps and flags of many world countries, with lots of facts and geographic information as well.

www.un.org—Complete information on the workings of the United Nations and information on its 191 member countries. The children's site— www.un.org/Pubs/CyberSchoolBus—has lots of interesting activities and information for kids.

www.usgs.gov—The official site of the U.S. Geological Survey contains lots of information on earthquakes, volcanoes, and other geological events worldwide.

www.worldbank.org—The site of the World Bank, an international organization dedicated to eliminating world poverty, has a kids' site that features a quiz and other information.

www.wri.org—The site of the World Resources Institute, an organization that provides information about global environmental problems.

www.your-nation.com—A site that lets you compare statistics for any two world countries.

INDEX

Page numbers in *italics* indicate maps or illustrations.

166   INDEX

Bolivia, 16, 57, 58, 60, 64–65
Bollywood, 93
Bombay (Mumbai), India, 25, 91, 93
borders, 19, 21, 42
Brasília, Brazil, 64
Brazil, 16, 19, 21, 22, 57, *58*, 59, 60, 63–64
bridges, longest suspension, 33–34
Buddhism, 30, 101, 102
Buenos Aires, Argentina, 64
buildings, tallest, 33, 39

C
cacao, 60
caldera, 120, 158
California, 43–44, 46, 47, 48
Cambodia, 102
Cameroon, 118
Canada, 8, 11, 18, 19, 30, 36–45, *38*
carbon dioxide, 31, 63, 118
car drivers, 90, 117–18
car emissions, 31–32, 51
Central America, *36, 49,* 51–54, 58
children, 64, 109
Chile, 54, 57, 60, 61, 65, 66
  earthquake, 12, 14
China, 90, 93–94, 96–100, *97*
  languages, 29, 30
  longest river, 16, 98
  population, 21, 22, 24, 42, 91, 96, 97
chocolate, 60
Christianity, 30, 70, 86, 88–89, 113
Chunnel, 75
cities
  ancient Aztec, 51
  most populous, 25–27, 39, 46, 48, 64, 78, 91, 101
  oldest inhabited, 88
climate, 35, 39, 69–70
CN Tower (Toronto), 39
coal, 60, 64, 99
coastlines, 9, 19
coffee, 59
cold, 18, 130, 132
Colombia, 11, 16, 21, 53, 57, 59–61
Columbus, Christopher, 55, 61
Communist governments, 80, 81, 100
computers, 33
Congo, 119
Constantinople, 87

continental drift, 5
continental shelf, 9
continents, 3, *4*, 5
  characteristics, 36, 67
  plates, 3, 11, 12, 43–44
copper, 59, 60, 65, 115
coral reefs, 51, 88, 128–29, 158
cork, 77
corn, 28, 45
Costa Rica, 51, 54
Côte d'Ivoire, 113–14, 118
countries, 18–25
  in Africa, 107
  in Europe, 70
  landlocked, 21, 64
  list of, 134–57
  in Middle East, 83, 110
  nations vs., 28
  in Oceania, 123, 125
  richest, 31
  in South America, 57
  states within, 27
  world's largest, *20*
cyclones, 94, 159

D
Damascus, Syria, 88
dams, 98–99, 110–11
Danube River, 67
Darwin, Charles, 61
Dead Sea, 89
Death Valley, 43
delta, 158
democracy, oldest, 80
Denmark, 35, 45, 71, 72, 73
desert, 17, 60, 65, 83, 85, 91, 109–10, 115, 121, 127, 158
dialect, 29, 71, 91, 158
diamonds, 115, 121
Djenne (Mali) mosque, 113, *114*
dodo bird, 120

E
earth, 6, 9, 11, 18
  age of, 8
  tilt of, 17, *18*
earthquakes, 3, 12, 33, 158, 160
  Central America, 52
  Japan, 100–101